W9-CPN-620

GET IN THE BOAT:

A JOURNEY TO RELEVANCE

p.187: UNCONSCIOUS FEAR IS FATE - CONSCIOUS IS RISK

PAT BODIN WITH ROBERT SCHAFFNER

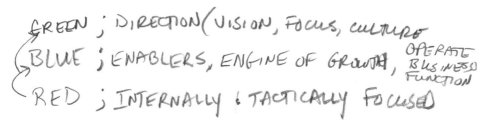

GREEN ; DIRECTION (VISION, FOCUS, CULTURE
BLUE ; ENABLERS, ENGINE OF GROWTH, OPERATE BUSINESS FUNCTION
RED ; INTERNALLY & TACTICALLY FOCUSED

Get in the Boat: A Journey to Relevance

© 2018 Pat Bodin. All rights reserved.
Printed in the United States of America.

ISBN-10: 1-946203-20-3
ISBN-13: 978-1-946203-20-5

—Disclaimer—

Although the author and publisher have made every effort to ensure
that the information in this book was correct at press time, the author
and publisher do not assume and hereby disclaim any liability to any party
for any loss, damage, or disruption caused by errors or omissions,
whether such errors or omissions result from negligence, accident,
or any other cause.

Paperback
Expert
www.PaperbackExpert.com

Table of Contents

DEDICATION

For Chrissy, my wife of 30 years.
Life with you is always a relevant journey.

FOREWORD

I wish I'd read this book at the beginning of my career – or even 20 years ago.

Let me step back and share how Pat and I first met. We met when we were both presenting at a conference a few years back. Pat was just fleshing out the Impact Framework, a system to easily understand people and their roles, and he and I had a lively discussion about Green, Blue, and Red people and their roles in a company. I have to admit that I didn't quite get it at first. I interpreted the colors as representing a specific meaning for each role. I mean, of course I wanted to be Green. They are the decision maker. Everyone wants to be Green, and the Blue person just sounded like a bore, so I wouldn't want to be him. Red is always bad, right? It means "stop".

Pat bluntly informed me that I had it all wrong. The colors weren't symbolic or significant – they were just shorthand for the roles they play. Green = Decision Maker. Blue = Business Enabler. Red = Product Producer. He said if it helped, I could assign any color to any role. Purple, Gold, and Platinum would work just as well. The essential point was that there are three basic roles, and each of these roles is necessary to the success of a company. For example, without the Red people, nothing would get done. You'd just have a bunch of Green and Blue folks sitting around talking. All the Colors are good, if done well.

I started to understand the message, but I still privately thought, "Well, sure, but I still want to be the Green guy."

When I read Pat's book, however, I realized that, though I understood the concept of the roles, I hadn't quite grasped the importance of the framework in which they operated. As I sat in the lounge of my hotel in Melbourne, you would have thought I was reading a thriller or some kind of comedy. I was absolutely absorbed by the material. I finally appreciated the significance of the colors and why it is important to know not just what role you are playing, but also what role the person you are working with or for is playing.

Knowing *the* role *tells you how to relate to the person you are talking to.*

Think about that for a second. At the end of the day, we don't do business with companies, we do business with people. In any negotiation or discussion, there is simply a person on the other side of the table, and your goal is to find out what you can do for that person – how you can be relevant. One of my favorite quotes from Pat is, *"Be interested – not interesting."* The goal is always to understand the objectives of the person sitting across the table. Never be afraid to ask the simple question, *"What does a good day for you look like?"* Let's be honest, other people aren't truly interested in what you are saying unless it is making their world better in some way. If you can find a way to the person on the other side of the table – a way to contribute to the growth of their company – you're relevant. The easiest way to do that is to simply ask what they need.

Years ago, I went to my company's Senior Sales leader and said, "I don't know exactly how we're going to do this, but I know what outcome I want. What are the top ten accounts this quarter and how can we (IT) help you grow them?"

I guess he saw my passion and sincerity for the project because he gave me the green light.

And then he gave me stock. In advance.

Understand what I'm saying because this is a big deal in my world. He gave me a bonus before I had produced a single thing. I cannot tell you how great it made me feel to be rewarded by the client – to have his confidence. It meant more than the stock reward – just knowing that he was backing my idea was huge.

Years later, I found myself in a similar meeting with Sales leadership. I had a good working relationship with the lead guy because I had consistently delivered on my promises to his organization. He had half an hour to hear my proposal and I spent the first 20 minutes telling him in detail what our organization did, how much collateral we generated, and how we delivered content – basically, how much work we were doing for the company. I could tell that he was just waiting for the time to pass until he could be out of our meeting. He was probably making a grocery list in his head while the minutes ticked by.

I got to the last 5 minutes of our meeting – the part where I talked about how we were driving growth and how we had developed a program that placed an IT advisor on all of his top accounts. My main message was that that my team had their backs. The guy completely lit up. I had his full attention as I described the plan in that few minutes and I realized that I should have started our meeting by discussing growth and the IT Advisor program without all the technical preamble. We could have spent the majority of our time really discussing how best to partner and make these efforts successful.

You see, this guy didn't care about anything but customer success and growth. Well, I'm sure he cared about his family and world peace, but in his work, his top priority was growing the business. He simply doesn't need additional information. Our relationship has grown leaps and bounds since these interactions because he knows that we share a common goal. Once I started

BE RELEVANT

speaking to the outcome he was trying to drive, we were speaking the same language.

This is the fundamental reason that technologists are rarely invited to have a seat at the table: We are not effective at communicating our relevance to leadership. We have developed our own jargon and defined our own processes in isolation. When we come to the table for the discussion, we are speaking an almost completely different language from the rest of the people at the table. I mean, for example, we use the word "virtualization" all the time, but there is literally no translation for that word in *any other language on the planet.* That's because it is only meaningful to technologists. No one outside of our discipline has a true understanding of it. We also think that the hard stuff we do is what we need to tell people about because these things take the most time and effort. The truth is, the other people at the table just need to know how we can help them get where they want to go. We need to be asking them *"What are your goals and how can we help you achieve them?"* Further, we need to be able to express ourselves in a common language.

I have an employee on staff who is a super technologist, just incredible. They can talk "Speeds and Feeds" to anyone in purely technical terms, but they are also able to explain tremendously technical processes in a practical way to people who don't need to know precisely HOW something is done. This is the sort of communication style that technologists need to learn.

Pat and Robert's Impact Framework gives us a methodology for doing just that. They offer a means of getting to the table and for being a part of the discussion once we get there. That's what made this book such an exciting read for me. It was a clear, quantifiable explanation of what I had seen in action over the course of my career.

I do wish I'd had this book 20 years ago, but I also find it very useful right now. It's a book for any stage of your career, and those of you at the early part of your career are doubly fortunate. You will have the insight and tools it has taken me decades to acquire. Read the book with an open mind and get ready to learn about principles you can put it into practice right away to become a key asset in your organization.

Use this book. Utilize the Impact Framework. Be wildly successful.

Lance Perry,
Vice President
Customer Strategy and Success
Cisco Systems

INTRODUCTION

I'm a hard-wired technologist. I'm proud of what I know. In a more revealing moment, I might even admit that my technical competency is where I find security. Over 30 years ago, I started my career in public accounting, but it wasn't good enough just to be an accountant – I had to be a CPA (Certified Public Accountant). When I went into computer engineering and worked for a few Fortune 100 companies, most notably Cisco Systems, I sought the most thorough and prestigious certification available at the time, the CCIE (Cisco Certified Internetworking Engineer). My goal, though I would probably have not admitted to it, was to be the smartest guy in the room and to have the credentials and experience to back it up. I felt my work, by virtue of my knowledge and experience, had meaning and importance. Boy, was I misguided!

Over the years, I found that expertise was simply not enough for satisfaction in my work. I enjoyed creating something from nothing. I liked the challenge of solving a problem someone else considered unsolvable. This is at the heart of why I was drawn to IT. It is a difficult, ever-changing world of problems requiring complex solutions and creative innovations delivered on almost impossible timelines. However, once I had mastered infrastructure technology, I was ready to move on to a new challenge: training others to master IT – architecting it, selling it, and using it.

I created Firefly, a technology training company, in 2003 as an answer to the biggest problem I saw with typical technology education. IT training made a lot of paper experts, but few people with real expertise. I believe this came from trainers who tended to have little to no experience at actually doing what they were teaching and from course curricula that favored marketing over practice. My company solved this lack of experience by combining professional services (mentored implementations) with the absolute best technical training available and became wildly successful because of that. After 10 years, Firefly had become a global success and it was time for me to move on to the next thing, so I sold it to a European consortium and took a few months off to chase down my next challenge.

I had been toying with an idea, just a thought, really, about what makes work meaningful. I knew that I was happiest in my work when I felt like what I was doing had meaning and it wasn't a question of how much money I was making or how much I could prove I knew, but of how I was using my knowledge to solve problems and create new concepts. That was clearly part of my satisfaction with my work, but I wondered if that was the path to a happier professional existence for everyone. I began my quest for an answer by reading, of course. I really enjoy concepts conveyed in a narrative, and my favorite writer of business narratives is Patrick Lencioni. His most famous book is The Five Dysfunctions of a Team: A Leadership Fable, but the one that really had an impact on my life is The Three Signs of a Miserable Job: A Fable for Managers. In "Three Signs", Lencioni declares that you must know the people you work with and you must be able to measure what you do, two things I believe most corporations lack. What really captured my attention and imagination, though, was the assertion that you must have relevance. Lencioni says, basically, that you're not relevant because of what you do, but because what you do affects other people.

The moment I read this, it became crystal clear that in technology and in STEM (Science, Technology, Engineering, and Mathematics) professions, relevance begets meaning. You become meaningful in your work because you are relevant in how you impact other people. So, as a technologist, how do you communicate the relevance of what you do to your organization? How do you decrease the friction between the technologist and the business leader or customer so things can happen faster and better? Can you answer the question of why you do what you do in the context of what your company provides its customers? How do you even get a seat at the table?

In the past, the downside of not including the technologists in business decisions was less severe because changes were few and spread out over time. Today, though, our businesses are experiencing change at speed and businesses can't afford to make decisions without their technologists in the mix. *The paradox is that while Technology is more important than it has ever been, technologists are often still kept at arm's length from business decisions and discussions.* This is the crux of the problem that this book seeks to solve.

I think of it like whitewater rafting. The business leaders are in the first boat. They are reading the river to determine the best route, while the technologists are being towed behind, picking up oars or coolers that the passengers in the first boat may have dropped. This setup may work well enough when running down Class 2 rapids, but today's businesses are running at Class 5 speeds, and towing the technologists in a separate boat is impractical and downright dangerous. There have been several companies over the past few years that have ended up with damning coverage in the Wall Street Journal due to the disconnect between the business leaders and technologists, especially in areas like cybersecurity breaches. We need a better way. We need the technologists to "Get in the Boat" with the business leaders to mitigate the daily challenges in real time and not purely in a reactive mode. It is imperative that organizations perceive technologists as relevant to the ongoing success and health of the business.

During a business trip to Munich about a decade ago, a colleague took me to Octoberfest where he introduced me to Robert Schaffner. I found a kindred spirit in Robert. Like me, he was striving to find meaning in work, and in 2013, we found ourselves in Paris at the same time, having lunch at my favorite restaurant on the Bois de Boulogne. There, at Le Chalet des Îles, overlooking the pond, we sat talking about finding meaning and relevance in work for four hours over a very decent little rosé.

We spoke of our frustration with technology suppliers who often sold products without understanding the customer's real problem. We believe that great technology selling should always be about the customer's needs and not about just giving them another widget. Customers have problems and a great technology company provides solutions to those problems – not just the next new thing that the customer didn't know they needed. We discussed our concerns that companies generally fail to connect the dots between what their products provide and what the customer needs. Thus began our journey into relevance.

BE RELEVANT

Robert and I, along with our colleague Michael Pohl, spent the next four years creating the Impact Framework. Over those four years, we found that there is an opportunity for Technologists to value chain what they do and what the organization needs. We realized that there are actually psychological and sociological differences between technologists and business leaders and we had to find a means of bridging the gap. We struggled to find the right methodology. We tried different approaches and different business models and we drew on a variety of domain expertise. In the end, the final piece fell into place simply because I didn't feel sufficient in my knowledge.

It wasn't the business knowledge. I have that. I'm a CPA, and I've built successful businesses from scratch.

And it wasn't the engineering, the technology. That's been my home nearly my whole life.

Then, last year I went back to university (after too many years to count) to complete the Lean, Six Sigma Black Belt certification and that led me to the missing piece. What I was missing was the *process*. For instance, you can't actually deliver complex infrastructure technology directly to the business. You have to go through a framework to convey the relevance of the technology you are delivering. What we've done is create a framework that provides a systematic model you can use to be relevant. Every. Single. Time.

We have arrived at a way to teach you what you didn't learn when you were acquiring expertise in your field. What technologists and other STEM professionals are missing is the understanding of how to plug into an organization and connect the tangible (the things that you do) to the intangible (the thing your business needs or wants) through the business process and *how to communicate your relevance to your organization*.

The whole goal of this book is to teach technologists how to become enablers of the organizations they are in so they can have an impact on the organization. Once we become enablers, we will be seen as relevant, will be asked to join the leaders at the table, and we will find meaning in being part of something bigger than ourselves. That is what the framework is about.

Because, let's face it. If you don't find a way to be an enabler – a way to have a material impact — you become a tool, and the problem with being a tool is that you can be automated.

If you want to have a material impact on your company, this book is for you.

If you are a business leader who wants to know how to align your company resources to react quickly and productively to market changes, this book is for you.

If you are a supplier who wants to know how to be a good business partner and less of a discount warehouse, this book is for you.

If you are a technologist or other STEM professional who wants to know how to be relevant to your organization and how to communicate that relevance effectively to business leaders, vendors, or customers, this book is for you.

Is change worth the risk?

This book asks you to change. That raises a question: *Will this change be worth the risk?* Some of you might be tempted to maintain the status quo because you aren't sure the future will be any better. You may assume that you have a limited time in your current position and that you'll just move on when this stage comes to an end. You may not feel an incentive to put in hard work and get back…what? What exactly will you get back? You're not sure. You may feel content to clock in, do the job your boss asks of you, clock out, and repeat the next day.

Is change worth the risk? Let me answer that with a few other questions. Are you satisfied with your job? Does your work have meaning? Are your daily activities imbued with significance? Do you feel relevant? Job satisfaction, meaning, significance, and relevance all come from using your abilities to positively impact others and your organization. You can keep trudging along, doing what you do—but isolated from the bigger picture, you'll be neither relevant nor satisfied. You'll always know you could have had something more.

A Technologist can be relevant. They can be an integral part of your organization's success. They should join business leaders in the main boat to help them navigate obstacles and steer toward triumph.

Is the benefit of change worth the risk? I certainly think so.

Why don't you come along on this journey and see for yourself?

Pat Bodin

* WORKING WITH LEADERSHIP. BUILD THE SLOW DIVISION

SECTION I.

How Business Works

Chapter 1.

What's Around the Bend?

Rapid change is making life hard for technologists and this change carries inherent risk. Should we swap non-cloud services for cloud services? Risk. How should we direct the company? Risk. Massive sea changes are happening. What's more, the speed of those changes is increasing exponentially.

Consider something with which we are familiar: vacations. We travel much differently today than we used to. Twenty years ago, planning a vacation required a visit to your local travel agent. You would drive to the office, sit down in front of the agent's desk, browse through catalogs, and the agent would dial up flight options on their computer. Today, planning a vacation may involve sitting at your kitchen table while still in your pajamas, reading reviews on Trip Advisor, booking a room on Airbnb, and checking flight options on applications such as Hipmunk or Kayak for the best deals.

You can generalize these observations about change to almost any other organization. The trend began in the 1990s in high-velocity areas like Wall Street financials and it just hit Main Street in the last decade. Want proof of the trend? In the 1920s, the average public company had a 67-year life expectancy. Today, that lifespan is 15 years.[1] Business is rife with uncertainty.

Leadership within a business often causes change. Major shifts by the people who lead an organization affect the company's direction. However, those changes aren't always obvious to the employees downstream. This disconnect creates uncertainty because technologists don't know why leaders are altering course—they may not even realize anything has happened.

Technologists strive to use technology to promote business goals. However, if no one is telling them that the entire organization has changed course, they will likely be directing technology decisions toward an outdated goal. Time and resources will be wasted and the business will be thwarted in reaching its objectives.

In a Different Boat

I don't know if change will continue at this tumultuous pace. It may not be sustainable. But for the time being, we must manage hundreds of decisions that could go awry.

Think of it like white water rafting on a highly turbulent Class 5 rapid. Every decision you make now affects later decisions. If

---

[1] Vijay Govindarajan and Hylke Faber, "How Companies Escape the Traps of the Past," Harvard Business Publishing, accessed November 13, 2017. https://hbr.org/2016/04/how-companies-escape-the-traps-of-the-past.

you decide to paddle right to avoid a boulder, you may find a new obstacle awaiting you. You don't know what the next rapid will be like—a whirlpool may throw you into the water! That is the uncertain future and technologists are bearing the worst of it.

For various reasons, the technologists have been kept at arm's length from the business. You might think they'd be able to sit alongside the business leaders, notice an upcoming rapid, and alter course together. Why can't they? Because *they're not in the same boat*. They've been placed into another boat that trails along behind.

The Paradox

Here's the paradox: as I survey my career of over 30 years, technology is more relevant than it has ever been and yet *technologists are still kept at arm's length from business decisions and discussions*. I find it interesting that technology has become highly important while the person who is supposed to be managing the technology has become a roadblock. In fact, technologists are almost *universally* perceived as roadblocks. How do I know? I did a sampling.

Over two and a half years, I interviewed 750 businesspeople, simply asking, "What do you think of IT?" Before the interviews, I expected to have some negative responses. What I never expected was an utter lack of positive reviews! Out of 750 interviews, 750 responses were negative. "We don't like IT. IT is a roadblock. IT is in our way." Yet, when I asked for them to give me an example of how IT specifically was a roadblock to them, at least 70% of the people I spoke with could not provide me with one.

I believe this indicates a lack of understanding and a lack of communication with those in IT. People in the business functions—those who do sales, marketing, engineering—don't know what the technologist is doing. Moreover, they don't communicate what they are doing to the technologists. Both sides are mutually ignorant of the other.

Since the technologists are unaware of the business functions' requirements, they spend an exorbitant amount of time studying what new capabilities to develop for the business, but often by the time they reach a conclusion, the needs of the business have changed. This is a massive disconnect. Change happens in the business while the technologists are still hard at work trying to implement the last change, which is often a capability that has already become obsolete and irrelevant.

What's the issue? *They're not in the same boat.* If functional leaders and technologists were sitting together in the same boat, they would all be able to see the upcoming rapids at the same time. They could navigate around rocks and branches and whirlpools together. They could change in unison and work as a team. To face an uncertain future with confidence, technology leaders need to get in the lead boat along with business leaders.

The negative reviews

Earlier, I shared my experience of asking business leaders what they thought of IT. I'd like to return to that experience, but also let you in on the story behind it.

Some years ago, I was sitting with a senior vice president of one of the largest chemical companies in the world. This man, a few years shy of 70, oversaw the American operations. During our conversation I asked, "So what do you think of technologists?" He proceeded to say, "I love technologists! They are so fantastic."

I was surprised, because most business leaders are not so enthusiastic. I inquired, "What do you mean?" "Well, Pat, one of the many things we do is paint cars for automobile manufacturers. When I started in this industry, we had to have a thousand cars come off the assembly line with the same color—because we couldn't cure the color back then. We had no tools to be able to change colors on the assembly line, so the solution was to paint a long series of cars the same color. Today, because of our technologists, we can paint cars with custom colors quite easily. If you buy a car in London with a paint job in your favorite color, then wreck that car in Germany, we can repaint the car there with precisely the same color. Technologists have enabled our business to offer some incredible features."

As he spoke, I realized that when he said "technologists" he was talking about product engineering. So, I continued, "Okay. Now, what do you think of IT?" And the VP went from total excitement to total despair. (Sometimes I exaggerate my stories to make a point, but this time I'm not.) He said to me, "Pat, we're never going to solve our issues with IT."

That conversation made me think, "I should ask other business leaders what they think of IT." So, I began collecting data, and over the past two and a half years whenever I found myself speaking to a functional leader outside the IT department, I would say, "In general, what do you think of IT?"

I thought the answers would be mainly negative, but I wanted to be hopeful. Never did I expect that in two and a half years not one person would give me a positive response. One person initially answered positively, but then I asked, "Great! Why are you positive toward IT?" He chuckled and said, "Well, I'm not sure. I want to be positive, but last week they messed up our ERP system and we couldn't sell for an entire week." *Out of 750 people, not one positive response.*

My follow-up question was, "Why do you have this negative outlook on IT?" And 70% of businesspeople could not give me a precise reason. I find that very interesting. It tells me that highly intelligent and highly competent IT people who brainstorm ingenious ways to solve business problems *are not viewed as part of the team.* They feel like lone wolves; they struggle with communication. Thus, the functional leaders have come to view them as obstacles and not enablers.

What happened?

How did this situation come to be? How long have technologists and business leaders been in different boats?

I enjoyed watching *Hidden Figures*, a movie about female, African-American scientists who helped NASA put a man on the moon. The women were whiz mathematicians and their job title was "computer". Yes, back in those days, a "computer" was a human being who was skilled at math. The first electronic computer imitated those human computers' abilities. Soon, we had the advent of the mainframe and then in 1964, we had the IBM 360, the first general-purpose computer, a central processing unit. For the next 20 years, those large computing devices lived within a function of the business, such as operations or engineering. Data processing belonged to a function and was not generally a shared service.

Let's say you work at an airline in 1976. Your job is to book airfare for customers and you need computing devices to process those transactions. However, if you wanted to communicate with the customer, you would either need to type and mail a letter or place a phone call and hope they were there to receive that call, as answering machines were not yet in home use. Likewise, other business functions generally had no computing devices at all. Sales? Doubtful. Marketing? Probably not. They had physical paper and typewriters, but not data processing.

Data processing came first to functions that handled transactions, such as payroll and taxes. Engineering also used computers when they needed to calculate something faster than a human computer could. Before 1981, technology assets were decentralized among the functions of the business. Everyone either had their own computing systems to do their own, specific job or they had nothing at all.

The advent of the IBM PC in August 1981 was a game changer. When the PC came on the scene, it provided increasing freedom from the typewriter and gave access to computers to more functions in the business who previously had none. By the mid-1980s, the PC was widespread in the business world and there were many business applications written for the PC. Increasingly, accountants no longer had to reconcile statements by hand, clerks didn't need to retype letters they made mistakes on, and managers were able to type up their own reports. It was at this time that technology assets which were once decentralized in their own departments began to be centralized for efficiency and supportability. By 1990, Microsoft was able to collapse the needs for word processing, spreadsheets, and slide sharing into one usable, friendly, functional tool; Microsoft Office. With Office, everyone in the organization could use a shared set of tools. Likewise, there were other suppliers that helped to consolidate and centralize the IT needs in communication, manufacturing, supply chain, and a myriad of other areas. This furthered the

OFFICE (1990) - CHANGED THE IT WAS VIEWED

pull toward IT centralization and the technologists were separated into their own department. The goal of IT centralization was to efficiently share assets but the unfortunate result was IT isolation.

So, IT centralization has not always been the status quo. Formerly, the tool was closer to the business functions—in fact, it was inside that function. But during the mid-1980s and 1990s, that tool became a shared service. Over the last 20 years, the IT department has lived outside of the function it serves, whether sales, marketing, product engineering, or anything else.

What's the problem with that? The problem is that speed has now increased in the functions to such a rapid pace that sharing resources is no longer practical. If the entire organization is sharing a resource, that resource may be too slow to react to any one particular business need in a certain function. Suppose you are the head of marketing and you've been charged with understanding exactly which customers you should send a promotion for a new product launch. Some of the data you would need would be contained in your ERP, CRM, and other systems and some of the data you need would be external. If you waited on the IT shared service to provide you with the data for this promotion, you may miss the product launch. As the marketing leader, you might create your own Data Analytics solution that looks at both the internal data about your customer and also the external data, so you could make the right decision in a timely fashion.

As a reaction to this problem, the pendulum is now swinging away from centralization toward decentralization. Decentralizing those assets may seem less efficient. However, the non-shared assets become free to support the specific needs of the particular business unit, which actually improves effectiveness.

The emergence of new assets in technologies has furthered decentralization by helping business functions to handle technology themselves; smartphones and tablets put control back into the hands of the user. Cloud and SaaS-based solutions (Dropbox, for instance) let the user demand the application logic, not depend on a centralized asset for that logic. Business functions embraced DIY and stopped relying on the shared service as much.

Not all technologists are supportive of this shift. Some younger technologists resist decentralization because they don't realize that a centralized technology organization hasn't always been around. Since they are only in their 20s or 30s, many presume centralization has been around for eons, not just the last 25 years. Others believe that technology decisions are best left in the centralized IT department who are most capable of managing those assets. They often react in fear like Chicken Little ("The sky is falling!") calling this newfound independence "Shadow IT" or "Rogue IT" in an effort to resist and delegitimize it. They must realize that decentralization is not the end of life as we know it, but rather an intelligent effort to connect technology to function and make sure we are in the same boat.

To summarize, the shared asset became slow and extremely disconnected from the functions of the business. Then, due to technological advances, the business functions decided they could handle matters themselves. The IT department resisted, but the business could not afford to depend on shared services that did not react to their specific needs. The functions couldn't wait anymore. The desire for efficiency was outweighed by the need for speed.

That's why the technologists are in a different boat. They are thoroughly disconnected from the business functions and the functions are trying to solve problems on their own.

Decentralization

Good Book!

One of my favorite books is <u>The Phoenix Project: A Novel About IT, DevOps, and Helping Your Business Win</u> by Gene Kim, Kevin Behr, and George Spafford. It's a novel about DevOps, which is an integration of Development with IT Operations. Basically, DevOps practitioners want to "get in the boat" with the business leaders. Their pitch to the leaders is, "You tell us what you need. The developers and IT operations will execute simultaneously." The question is: how do you get Development and IT Operations to walk in lockstep?

As <u>The Phoenix Project</u> opens, the company Parts Unlimited has problems. One is that IT is operating as usual. Technologists are in a vacuum and not enabling business success. Major projects are failing and the competition is outflanking them. "Project Phoenix" is supposed to be a breakthrough, but it has been in development for three years, gobbling up time and money.

The solution for Parts Unlimited was to integrate the components of their business together. The company dealt with many continuous improvement issues, especially the theory of constraints (see Eli Goldratt's *The Goal*). How do you deal with constraints in the system? How do you deal with workflow? How do you avoid rework? Parts Unlimited applied continuous improvement concepts to the development process and finally started delivering projects on time.

One character in the book is named Brent Geller a great example of a traditional IT guy. He is incredibly competent, but breaks as many things as he fixes, because he is out of sync with the business. That is a great representation of where IT is today. *(within IT)* What we need to do is get everyone in line toward continuous improvement in IT. Brent's boss, Bill Palmer, emphasizes continuous improvement to his Parts Unlimited team. Over time, IT becomes a core competency. Instead of a roadblock, IT becomes an enabler.

The Phoenix Project looks at decentralization through the lens of continuous improvement and DevOps. The book you're reading now has a complementary focus. *Get in the Boat* really concerns the role of every technologist and how they can be relevant to their organization and ultimately find true meaning in their work. Right now, the business leaders in our companies don't want technologists in the boat, because they believe they will create drag. This drag not only slows down the organization, but creates tension and friction between leadership and Technologists who actually do the work.

ASK; IS YOUR ORGANIZATION A DEZENTRALIZED OR COMTRALIZED ENVIRONMENT

Misconceptions

Dramatic change in IT is widespread, but this high-rate of change is uneven. Some companies have limited change due to the nature of their business and, for them, IT shared service works okay. Others are in such volatile markets or are so susceptible to security threats that change is required and our reactions to those changes are often haphazard and not well thought out. Once your organization has worked through the strengths and weaknesses of your current IT system, you will most likely find that not all IT functions can or should be decentralized. Some shared services are vital. Security is a prime example of the need for shared services. Security must be universal or the company will face peril. In fact, many organizations are elevating the data security into the executive management team and into the board of directors, since what is at stake is often the company's survival.

SHARED SERVICES (DECENTRALIZED)
  → SECURITY —
  ↪ DATA

For many companies today, *data is currency*. We use data to determine trends, seek new customers, and to comply with current government or industry regulations, and so much more. Customer data is needed by marketing, sales, product engineering, and additional functions; the whole organization needs access. Given the general need of the entire organization and the fiduciary responsibility to guard not only our own data, but our suppliers' and our customers' data, it is critical in most organizations that data be centralized. These are just a few examples of shared services that some have chosen to be centralized, but arbitrary centralization cannot be defaulted to any more simply because of efficiency. Too much is at stake.

Technologists get caught up in two misconceptions that keep them from being the enablers of the business they ought to be: efficiency and quality.

PROBLEM WITH IT DEPARTMENTS

"Efficiency Is King"

Efficiency is not king. Why? Because in this era of massive change, efficiency will not cause you to win in business. At the end of the year, your business will not survive because you were a little more efficient. The business will survive because it found a market with customers who are willing to pay. In the grand scheme of the organization, the rate of efficiency you bring to bear is so immaterial as to have almost no bearing. Especially when the lifespan of business survival is shrinking, your ability to save the business money over time is immaterial. You may be trying to save your company money over the next decade—but the company might not even be there in a decade.

Consider Amazon. Amazon is a margin vampire that sucks the life out of every industry it can sink its fangs into. The life of a company is their ability to deliver the product or service that a customer will purchase; the total amount of the customers' purchases is called Revenue or Turnover. Subtract revenue by the cost directly associated with producing that revenue and that's called *gross margin* or *operating income*. Gross margin is the lifeblood of a company. Amazon has done an amazing job of reaching both business and consumers in ways that no one else has, but what's really amazing is their ability to do that at such a low cost. Warren Buffett has called Jeff Bezos "The most amazing business person of our age!" What Buffett admires about Bezos is his ability to navigate a plethora of variables while constantly entering new markets and taking advantage of those markets using Amazon's incredible business model.

Amazon's business model is now attacking businesses far and wide and their large competitors are fighting back in unexpected ways. Amazon acquired Whole Foods in August 2017 and companies like Kroger, Waitrose, Walmart, and others are shaking in their boots. Walmart is now strategically approaching their suppliers and warning them, "Don't use Amazon Web Services (AWS). Switch to one of Amazon's competitors."[2] The suppliers' technologists think technology decisions should be based on efficiency, features and performance; they don't understand why their bosses just outlawed AWS. No one told them they cannot use AWS lest Walmart blacklist them, they just woke up and found out that their largest customer is forbidding use of one of their largest IT suppliers and it does not compute. Therein lies the disconnect.

---

[2] Dennis Green, "It's War: Walmart Is Telling Vendors to Stop Using Amazon's Cloud," Business Insider, accessed November 13, 2017. http://www.businessinsider.com/walmart-tells-its-tech-providers-to-stop-using-amazon-services-2017-6.

This whole layer of abstraction based on *business decisions* seems completely foreign to a technologist who thinks everything is based on a *technology decision*. He says, "This is the best tool!" But in the wider view of business health, the best tool varies according to business needs and in our example, the suppliers' relationship with Walmart outweighs AWS's superiority to alternative tools. These complexities are traditionally above the technologist's awareness level and technologists navigate them with difficulty.

"Quality Of Technology Matters Most"

Quality of technology has little bearing on business decisions. Until technologists understand the direction of the organization, their understanding of routers and switches and servers is nearly immaterial.

Let's now imagine that it's 1950 and you need the news of what is happening in the world. What is required to meet that need? You can read the morning and afternoon paper, you can turn on the evening news, and a newsreel may even play before you watch Elizabeth Taylor in "Father of the Bride" at the theater. Fast forward more than sixty-five years later to our current time, almost no one reads newspapers anymore, the movies don't play newsreels, and no one wants to wait for the evening news to find out what is transpiring in the world. Today, people get their news from websites, smartphone apps, social media, or they can tune in to a dedicated news channel on TV any time of the day. While the need for information is stable, the requirement changes.

Technologists have continued to design and provide technology for *requirements*. They often do not realize that the requirements have changed. That's not terrible, because the need is still present. But the challenge is to meet that need with different requirements in an ever-changing world. Technologists must understand the actual *needs* of their business and not the requirements, because the requirements will shift and today shifts take place in a matter of months or years, not decades. Technologists must be much more aligned to the core principles of their business and to what its functions need.

Since technologists have been relegated to a different boat than business leaders for some time now, they easily fall into the misconception that technology itself matters. It's as if the hammer woke up one day and thought, "The most important thing about me is the type of metal that forms me." That's not what matters most. What matters most is the *nail*. There is no *need* for a hammer without a nail and likewise there is no need for a technology solution without a business need. Technologists tend to think that tools have merit in and of themselves. In reality, they have no merit outside of the impact they can make on the business. When the means becomes an end in itself rather than a way to serve the company's corporate ends, the rest of the business considers technologists to be irrelevant.

Harvard professor Theodore Levitt says, "People don't want to buy a quarter-inch drill. They want a quarter inch hole." People run to the store to buy a drill bit not because they enjoy the aesthetic beauty of its spiral, not because they know the exact angle that the spiral is cut or the exact degree of sharpness on the edge, not because they enjoy owning steel, and not because they appreciate the history of the invention of the electric drill, but because of their need to get a quarter-inch hole in the wall. The hole is the *need* and the drill bit is the *requirement*. Knowing lots about drill bits and appreciating drill bits apart from the purpose of putting a hole in the wall is completely irrelevant.

This is the situation that technologists are in today: They know a ton about drill bits but have forgotten about the hole. That is why the functional leaders relegate them to a different boat.

The higher purpose: Enabling

What do the business functions care about? Being enabled to get their job done. That is the higher purpose of IT. Technologists often do not realize their inherent power to be enablers. Enablers are those who stand alongside business leaders, perceive coming changes, and facilitate the business to reach its desired outcomes through technology.

My friend and business associate Dave Yeary explains this idea well:

> *Whether you are new to the IT world or a seasoned veteran and whether you seek to expand your scope or are happy with the level of responsibility you have, you need to understand the role of IT. Doing so will make you better at what you do and reduce unproductive stress as you navigate your career. Simply put, IT exists only to support a company's quest to execute a successful strategy. Business leaders would not spend a dime on IT if they did not have to. Decades have proven that all companies leverage IT and successful companies leverage it to a great extent. So, if IT is extremely valuable, why do we need to do anything different? Lost opportunity is the answer.*
>
> *We all recognize Steve Jobs as a visionary. We recognize that he leveraged technology to execute his vision. Steve didn't*

concern himself with the details of the technology; he just believed it could be done. But, how might things have changed if he didn't have Steve Wozniak, the co-founder of Apple, in his life? Maybe he would have connected with a technologist and found a common language—or maybe not. The big question is "How many enlightened business minds have great ideas that are never executed because they don't know how to interface with the technology world?" We may never know. What we do know is that an entire generation of young people is growing up with an assumption that technology can do anything. There always seems to be "an app for that." I recently heard a father tell the story of how he was driving down the freeway with his young son, being buffeted badly by the wind. As a "mature" person, the father just battled the side forces and complained about the car. But his son, almost instinctively, spoke up and said "Dad, do you think there is an app that we can download to help the car deal with the wind?"

The journey to connect the unconnected has just begun and it will be an amazing journey. What is clear to me is that many opportunities will be missed if the people in the strategic business world are not able to communicate with those in the technology world. What is also clear to me is that the burden lies with the technologists to take the initiative, as it is a daunting task for the classic business mind to delve into technology.[3]

We technologists should think of ourselves as enablers. Once we are enablers of the business leaders, we will feel and be relevant. That feeling of relevance will bring a sense of achievement to our work. We will then be happier and more fulfilled human

---

[3] Personal communication between Dave Yeary and Pat Bodin, November 10, 2017.

beings. Are you not entirely sure how to do this? Don't worry—I have good news. Just keep reading and you'll learn.

Uncertainty and visibility

How do you turn an uncertain future into a more certain one? Well, the future can never be known exhaustively, but you can gain some certainty through *visibility*. You don't want to be trailing behind the main boat in another boat. Why? Because you experience all the negative aspects of the rapids yet never get credit for any of the positive. You are being dragged. The rapids will speed up, twist, and turn, but you will not have visibility to deal with these changes at the necessary speed. Until you get into the front boat, you will never enable the business to deal with this uncertain and disruptive environment. You cannot be aligned with the other leaders from the back.

We are not in control of the rapids, but we can be in control of where we sit in the boat, and therefore what we can see in the water. By being closer to the rapids and sitting alongside the organization's other leaders, technologists can grow in certainty of how to avoid being dumped into the water. The rapids will remain volatile, but your team will be prepared to navigate them with confidence. As you work together, you can react to upcoming obstacles with agility and effectiveness. The business really needs technologists to ride in the same boat as the other leaders. The IT leadership is essential to making good decisions—avoiding this rock and that whirlpool. It is imperative that they gain entrance to the main boat for the survival and growth of the company. How? That is what this book will teach you.

Chapter 2.

The Architecture of Your Business

How do you choose which restaurant to go to for dinner?

Robert Schaffner's story:

I've found that throughout the world, most everyone loves to go out to eat, enjoying one another's company and a good meal. Only once in my career have I met someone who said he didn't like to eat out. I asked him, "Well, what about if someone else is paying. Do you like eating out, then?" That changed his answer. What makes a good restaurant? What are the key criteria? Many will say it's such factors as the environment, wine list, food quality, price, and location. When I was in Jakarta, someone told me that the determining factor for eating out was location, because getting from central Jakarta to south Jakarta could take hours. What's interesting is that unless someone specifically has a taste for pizza from a wood burning oven or Pit BBQ, you could ask hundreds of people what the deciding factor is when choosing a restaurant and it would be exceedingly rare to hear back, "I look for the particular equipment they use in the kitchen." Can the kitchen infrastructure make a difference in the quality of the food preparation? Of course, but very few people would ever ask about the equipment when making a restaurant choice, although the kitchen infrastructure may come up peripherally if they are avoiding food allergens or keeping kosher, for instance. Kitchen infrastructure can be important for the quality of the food, which impacts the customer experience. Despite its importance, the customer does not say, "Bring me straight to the kitchen. I want to check which oven you have and how sharp your knives are." The kitchen infrastructure is essential but not interesting. The challenge in IT is similar. Technologists live in the "kitchen" behind the scenes. They are extremely important to the experience that customers working with their organizations have. But the technologist's way of thinking is not at all like the customer's way of thinking—the technologist speaks a language few understand.

What if the staff at a restaurant tried to sell their kitchen's dishes like IT people try to sell technology? Instead of saying "Enjoy our warm, delicious French onion soup," they would say "We use the newest model gas range oven, delivering instant heat with infrared elements for the fastest temperature recovery."

If you saw that advertisement as a customer, where they are touting their equipment instead of their food, what would you think? Would that make you want to dine there? I think it's safe to say that hearing about the technological details of the restaurant's oven would not make most people more inclined to go to that restaurant. It might even scare them away. They want to eat somewhere that has delicious soup, after all!

That is the reaction that IT gets when the technologists use language that no one understands, language which does not resonate with their customers. That is why our "restaurant" doesn't have many guests. Business leaders hear the technologist's presentation and think, "I have no clue what that means. I'd rather avoid this entirely." We need to understand how our customers think and who our customers are if we are going to be successful.

Three Tiers Of Business

[handwritten: —Strategy, operational, Tactical]

You can think about business architecture in three tiers. These tiers refer to people that belong to different organizational roles according to their responsibilities.

Tier one: Strategy

Tier One is **strategy.** Strategists provide direction to the organization. They provide the vision, the culture, and the focus. Ultimately, they are responsible for the business model of the organization.

(Fun fact: The word *strategist* comes from the ancient Greek word "strategos," meaning "general," as in a military leader.)

Often, the IT world refers to strategists as "lines of business". Strategists never refer to themselves that way, though, so the result is friction in communication. I'm not sure from whom or where in IT this practice originated, but it is very confusing. Recently, I was conducting a keynote presentation in south Florida when I asked a leader of a company what line of business he managed. I intentionally did it to show how our language can confuse others. He was a CPA like me and ran the financial and back office of a system integrator. After I asked him, he looked confused and struggled to say anything. I think his exact words were, "Hmm, I don't know. Let me think about that." I immediately asked him what function he managed and was responsible for and without hesitation he said, "Finance." There was absolutely no friction with that phrasing. It is a matter of respect to call people by the role they play and by which they actually refer to themselves in the industry instead of a generic, overly inclusive term like "lines of business," and it opens communication.

Reducing unnecessary friction is vital if you want to earn a spot in the lead boat. One way that I have found to reduce friction and understand more clearly the role a business leader plays is to ask them, as I did this CPA, what business function they lead. The director of sales isn't a "line of business" but rather is the functional leader of the sales department; the Chief Marketing Officer isn't a "line of business," but rather is the functional leader of marketing, and so forth. Use their language and hone your focus on what they do.

Now, there is such a thing as a "line of business" but it is not every business person. In a service organization, the head of sales for a region is responsible for that line (or territory of business). In a product manufacturer, the head of that particular product is responsible for that particular line. The people who actually refer to themselves as "line of business" is a narrow portion of the business people. You don't need to keep up with who calls themselves "line of business" – just ask them what function they have. They'll tell you.

The bottom line for strategists is that they provide the structure to the organization. Strategists captain the ship, pointing the rudder in the right direction.

Tier two: Operations

Operations is the engine that pushes the business forward. It includes the people, processes, and technology that propel the organization. Enabling is the job of Operations. The strategists create the plan and Operations enables the organization to fulfill it by implementing processes and policies. Operations desire to reduce friction with people and technology. Consider Apple, which sold 41 million iPhones in Q3 2017. With that high sales volume, they must eliminate friction in their supply chain, lest they fail to ship phones on time. Procedures and policies exist not as ends in themselves, but to reduce friction.

Most of an organization's employees are in Operations. They work in business processes and need to be aligned with corporate and regulatory policies. Thus, any change to existing business processes or policies has a direct impact on the Operations people. Each department in Operations has managers and leaders who are subordinate to the functional leaders and responsible to enable their strategy. Operations is the engine of the business.

Applications are vital to Operations. While it is true that strategists may need the use of email and business dashboards in their job, Operations core functionality requires applications to complete its job. In my observation, many people perceive that there are a few critically important applications and literally thousands of processes. This is not the case. There are hundreds to thousands of applications, depending of the size of the enterprise, and only a couple dozen or fewer processes. Many people are confused between the general process (Sales, Training, etc.) and the specific standard operating procedures (SOPs). It is kind of like the old adage about not seeing the forest for the trees; it is easy to get so caught up in looking at the trees (the SOPs) that we lose the sight of what is fundamentally the more important thing

– the forest (the process). When you look at the specific process (sales, manufacturing, supply chain, field service, etc.), it is best to use a macro level perspective, unless you have ownership and responsibility for the specific process. A micro level perspective provides little value to our understanding. The heart of the operational world is process and policy, the engine by which Operations enables the organization's goals.

Tier three: Tactical

The Tactical component of an organization provides support. Tacticians are internally focused and they supply the basic functionality that operators need do their job. For instance, tacticians manage the warehouses in the manufacturing supply chain. They handle the facilities where strategists and operators work. They provide the IT infrastructure. They set up phones and computers and networks.

Do companies need these tacticians? Yes, absolutely—they are key to success. Do tacticians need to be employed full time by the company? Not necessarily—they could be outsourced. Historically, many companies have done that, perhaps contracting with a third-party distribution center or outsourcing part of IT. But there is a disconnect between the operators and the outsourced company; the outside party may perform better than internal IT, but it is not as closely aligned with the goals of the business. The outsourcer's goal is to make money from the service. Unfortunately, that can cause innovation to stall or lead the outsourcer to charge for any small change that occurs outside the contract. This causes friction. Nevertheless, outsourcing of warehousing, facilities, and technology is becoming more commonplace. Since the operators are the ones receiving support, the fundamental question is, "What is the right decision for the operators and the organization?" Tacticians help operators get their job done.

How The Tiers Fit Together

How do the tiers fit together within an organization? You can think about them as three parts of a ship.

* Strategy – the captain
* Operations – the engine
* Tactical – the hull[4]

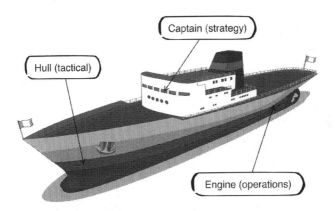

A ship's captain instructs his men to "Point the ship in this direction," which is precisely the job of the strategists. They should

---

4 "Ship" image (https://commons.wikimedia.org/wiki/File:Ship.svg) by Angelus (https://commons.wikimedia.org/wiki/User:ANGELUS) is licensed under CC BY-SA 3.0 (https://creativecommons.org/licenses/by-sa/3.0/). Desaturated from original; captions added.

set the rudder and then get out of the way so that the operators can work.

The engine propels the boat toward its destination, which is the task of the operators. They make the ship go.

The hull that supports the entire ship is like the tacticians who support the other two tiers. They keep the company from falling apart at the seams.

What is the ratio of strategists to operators to tacticians? Most organizations have only a few people in the Strategy tier. Commercial companies then have *many* operators with relatively *fewer* tacticians supporting them. Even if you want to be an enabler in Operations, you may find yourself in a tactician's role due to the nature of the organization.

Chapter 3.

Value Chaining

Do you like coffee? 400 billion cups of coffee are consumed globally per year, so if you do, you aren't alone. What do people like about coffee? Many people enjoy coffee's cultural aspects; Meeting up for coffee can be a nice, informal way for them to meet new people or get together with old friends; "Let's do coffee!" For some, coffee has become a habit – it's the way they wake up every morning; "Don't talk to me before my first cup of coffee!" Other people appreciate the chemical in coffee which allows them to focus whereas it would otherwise be difficult; "I need to drink coffee to be able to make my coffee!" And some people just like coffee's aroma, warmth, and flavor; "Mmmm. Coffee!"

Although these are all different benefits, they have a similar thread; they are intangible and often they are feelings. There are people in Brazil, the largest producer of coffee beans in the world, that know everything there is to know about the coffee bean, all of its tangible benefits and what features, qualities, and growing conditions make the best beans. Ultimately, however, a coffee bean has little use if it doesn't make its way into our coffee cup. This happens when we prepare the bean, a process which involves roasting, grinding and brewing. Interestingly enough, most end customers of coffee care very little about the bean itself, but care a great deal about the taste and the aroma produced by the bean. Connecting the tangible (bean) with the intangible (aroma, taste) through the process (roasting and grinding style, brewing device) is the key to great coffee.

¥ DISCONNECT BETWEEN TACTICIANS & STRATEGISTS

Connecting Coffee Beans To Intangible Value

If you want to make coffee, what is the primary ingredient? Coffee beans. You can find coffee beans at any grocery store, at that international coffee chain that's on every corner, and at your local, hipster coffee shop.

Some people care a lot about growing the bean—we might call them "coffee tacticians". They know the history of the bean (which, they may even correct you, is technically the seed of the coffee "cherry," rather than a bean), they know the climate and altitude it grows best in, its growing season, and they know when is the best time to harvest the bean for the fullest flavor. Coffee tacticians love nitty-gritty bean details.

On the other end of the spectrum, some people care little about beans. They only drink coffee for alertness, or morning ritual, or aroma, or social value. These "coffee strategists" focus on the *results* coffee offers. Coffee tacticians quickly bore them with discussions of organic, fair-trade, small-batch, high-flavor, low-something beans.

Coffee tacticians have very specific knowledge about beans. Coffee strategists have very specific desires that coffee can help them achieve. However, they communicate with each other poorly: The strategist asks the tactician for a cup of Joe and is forced to endure a bean lecture. The tactician asks the strategist for funds to support a small farmer and is surprised by the lack of interest. How do you connect the two together?

Enter the "coffee operator". He knows how to receive beans from the tactician, roast those beans, grind them, put them into a French Press or drip brewer or Keurig, and come out with the dark, flavorful brew that the strategist so desires. The operator selects a process that is *precise to the strategist's desire*. Does the strategist want nuanced flavor? French press. Convenience? Programmable drip brewer so that it's already brewed in the morning upon waking. Speed? Keurig is the way to go. The operator connects strategy and tactics.

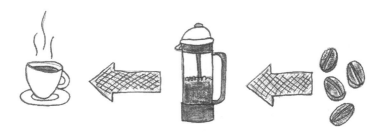

You may be a talented bean tactician who can grow the best coffee ever, yet be ignorant of (or just not care about) what happens after you package it and send it off to processing. There is a disconnect between your competency as a tactician and the needs of the business. Another disconnect occurs when the strategists' intentions get garbled as they flow down through the business tiers. In the end, everyone misunderstands and frustration ensues.

In the three tiers of business architecture, the level of Strategy is not precise. Up on the top level, the 50,000-foot view matters most. This is why John Sculley could change jobs from president of PepsiCo to CEO of Apple. It's why Alan Mulally could switch from CEO of Boeing to CEO of Ford. Airplanes and automobiles are totally different industries with diverse buying cycles, but the *strategy* is similar enough that a high-level executive can switch from one to the other. ← *strategist*

The challenge is that the speed of business is changing. According to the Harvard Business Review, "Half a century ago, the life expectancy of a firm in the Fortune 500 was around 75 years. Now it's less than 15 years."[5] For their business to survive, strategists must be able to quickly alter its course in response to market realities. The captain must call out course changes faster than ever before. Even so, the level of *precision to the company* is not high: executives can switch from the Department of Defense to Coca-Cola to the Cartoon Network. Their job is strategy, and while strategy is specific, it is not precise.

The same is true down in the Tactical world. Let's say you're a talented infrastructure network engineer—you can route packets anywhere given any protocol. You might work for Cisco today, a railroad next year, and an airline five years down the road. Your job is very specific, but not *precise to the company.*

 How do you connect the specific (but not precise) trajectory of the strategist to the specific (but not precise) tasks of the tacti-

---

[5] Govindarajan and Faber, "How Companies Escape the Traps of the Past."

cian? You use an operator. Zooming in on the second tier, this is where precision occurs.

OPERATIONS

Operators connect the specific goals of the strategists and the specific tasks of the tacticians with precision. Operators receive inputs from the tactician, then turn those into outputs that the strategists request. The output is the intangible benefit your organization offers. For instance, if you work in public safety, the intangible benefit is *feeling safe*. To accomplish that intangible result, you must do tangible procedures, like have a police car drive past a certain corner every 15 minutes. You need policies associated with those procedures, like "Turn on the body camera whenever a 911 call comes in." Precision dwells at the level of the operator. Operators connect tacticians to strategists. They identify a "value chain" that extends from the most nuts-and-bolts tactical activities all the way up to the stratosphere of strategic business planning.

Connecting Your Work To Business Value

To be relevant in your job, you must connect your work to business value. The job of IT is to manufacture technology and services for the functional leaders of the business. How do you connect your day-to-day work to the value your organization delivers to end users? *Value chaining* answers that question.

Michael Porter is a teacher at Harvard Business School, the most-cited scholar today in the fields of economics and business.[6] Originally introduced in Porter's book <u>Competitive Advantage: Creating and Sustaining Superior Performance</u>, the concept of the value chain expertly connects business *activities* to business *outcomes*. A value chain is "a set of activities that an organization carries out to create value for its customers."[7] Value chaining connects the dots between the activities of tacticians, operators, and strategists to show how value is created.

In the coffee value chain, beans go through a French Press to create flavor. The different parts of the value chain interrelate. If the goal is a hit of caffeine, the quality of beans is not so important. If the goal is a fantastic cup of coffee to serve a client while negotiating a deal, the quality of beans matters enormously. The tactician delivers value to the process not when he produces beans in a vacuum, but when he produces the right beans to hit the goal.

Here are some other value chaining examples.

SpaceX

Consider Elon Musk at SpaceX: his goal is Mars by 2024. His buyers are NASA and certain specialized businesses.

How will he achieve that? With increasingly advanced rockets, such as the re-usable ones SpaceX has now successfully landed back on earth after trips to space.

---

[6] According to his Harvard Business School faculty page, located at http://www.hbs.edu/faculty/Pages/profile.aspx?facId=6532.

[7] Mind Tools Content Team, "Porter's Value Chain," MindTools, accessed November 13, 2017. https://www.mindtools.com/pages/article/newSTR_66.htm.

What needs done to promote that *how*? A ton of very specific, technical, and tactical work.

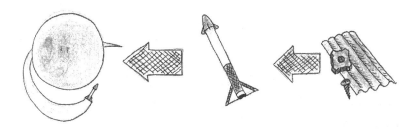

That's value chaining: connecting the dots between *what* and *how* and *why*.

Railroads

A U.S. railroad company can earn $800 million more revenue per year if they can increase the average speed of a cargo locomotive by 1 MPH. "Increase speed by 1 MPH" is a goal the railroads' strategists came up with.

If you know anything about railroads, you know the solution would not be to "push down on the gas pedal." Plenty of obstacles stand in the way of achieving that goal of increased speed: weight, timing, cycling issues, outdated technology. Enablers must analyze those and innovate *how* to increase speed. Then they hand specific projects to the tacticians so they can make improvements.

FitBit

Here's an example of a value chain in my personal life. I wear a Fitbit. It uses light pulses to track my heart rate, all day and all night. Since the Fitbit's design is unobtrusive, I feel comfortable wearing it all day. Fitbit's value chain looks like this:

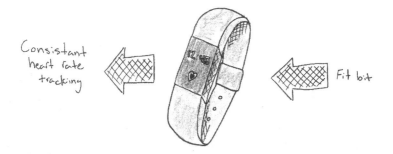

Consistant heart rate tracking ⇐ ⇐ Fit bit

When I work out, I use the Polar H10 heart rate sensor for more accurate heart rate tracking. This is a chest strap that uses electrocardiograph (EKG) technology to measure electrical impulses created by the heart as it beats. The value chain is similar, but slightly different:

Accurate heart rate tracking ⇐ ⇐ Polar H10

① What do you do at your business? ② What process are you involved in? ③ What value does that process create? Answer those questions and you're on the way to identifying your own value chain.

① ACCOUNT MANAGER / SALE
② BUSINESS DEVELOPMENT / RELATIONSHIP MANAGEMENT

③ CM

Communicating value in real-life encounters

Robert Schaffner's Story:

A friend of mine began his career selling Segways. He thought his product was fantastic, but he lived in a village in the countryside where the need for Segways is somewhat limited. He explored the region to find out who might benefit from one. He thought of a large car manufacturer in Bavaria—you might be able to guess which one. 'How can I gain entrance to that company?' he asked himself.

A contact of his who worked at the company gave him a tour of the plant. He noticed that the assembly line was very long, so he asked, 'Say there's a problem at one end of the production line and the engineer you need to solve the problem is at the other end. How long does it take him to walk from one end to the other? How much does that cost you?'

My friend learned that the engineer might need 10 minutes to walk the whole distance and 5 minutes to fix the problem. A production line pause of 15 minutes costs thousands of dollars—more than the Segway's price of a few thousand. My friend's question led to a purchase of about 20 Segways in order to reduce that 15-minute fix time to 8–10 minutes.

The point of that example is that you need to understand what people care about. Only then will your offer resonate with them. My friend connected the features of his product to the benefit it delivered—he identified a value chain. You can do the same.

Value chaining helps tacticians communicate the value of their job to higher-ups. See, most tacticians tend to think their work is *inherently valuable* inside a vacuum. Maybe a tactician is talented at configuring P2P on a public internet connection. Unfortunately, that by itself has *no value to the organization* and the intangible benefit it aims to deliver. The problem is compounded by the stark reality that many tacticians cannot even communicate what that intangible benefit is supposed to be.

One of my friends used to run IT infrastructure for a large IT manufacturer. He shared one of his goals with me: If his network engineers were to get in an elevator with the CEO, he wanted them to be able to carry on a relevant conversation for those 45 seconds. Typically, the CEO, being a strategist who focuses on intangibles, would start out with something like, "What do you do here?" Most network engineers, being tacticians who focus internally on tangibles, would reply, "My job is to configure a P2P router from here to New York City. My challenge right now is configuring the VPN tunnel between the two, because the configuration is giving me problems."

If you were in the elevator with them, you would have just witnessed a language breakdown, almost as complete as if the conversation partners were speaking in completely different languages with no translator present. What would be the result? The CEO would stop truly listening—though he may continue to look attentive just to be polite—and would become quite ready for the elevator to reach his floor. The tactician has created boredom rather than a positive impression. When the tactician's department asks for additional funding a few months later, the CEO is predisposed to regard his request as irrelevant to the goals of the business: "Why can't we just outsource the whole thing?"

Instead, the tactician was coached to translate his work into a benefit: "I work in communications. If I do my job right today, your New York City sales office will be operational tomorrow." Those simple words positively impact the strategist's perception of his company's tacticians. Tacticians can learn to communicate like that. It's not easy and requires a behavior change, but it's doable and it's important.

In the example of the elevator conversations, the first interaction was missing an *interface*. Tacticians can make an Ethernet connection and a T1 connection interface—but they seldom realize that language requires the same thing. Jargon must be translated into the strategist's language, thereby communicating value and reducing friction. Strategists really do want partners in the lead boat. If the tactician can demonstrate how they contribute to the company and make the strategist's job easier, the strategist will eventually invite the tactician to get in the boat. Low friction enables rapid response; together in the boat, they can see the upcoming rapid and work in unison to avoid it. Reducing friction between the three tiers inherently reduces risk and increases opportunity.

Value Chain
1. Feelings (waking up)
2. Process (french press)
3. Product (coffee beans)

Get in the Boat Whiteboard

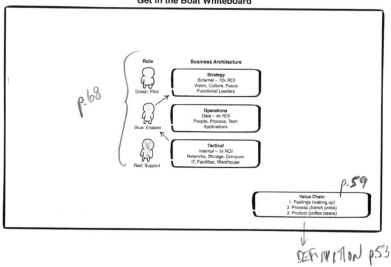

p.68

Role

Business Architecture

Green: Pilot

Strategy
External – 10x ROI
Vision, Culture, Focus
Functional Leaders

Blue: Enabler

Operations
Data – 4x ROI
People, Process, Tech
Applications

Red: Support

Tactical
Internal – 1x ROI
Networks, Storage, Compute
IT, Facilities, Warehouse

p.59

Value Chain
1. Feelings (waking up)
2. Process (french press)
3. Product (coffee beans)

DEFINITION p.53

SECTION II.

HOW PEOPLE WORK

Chapter 4.

The Color of Business

Some years ago, I realized that I needed an easier way to communicate about the people in the different business tiers. So, I color-coded them Red, Blue, and Green. There is no hidden agenda in the colors I chose.

p. 43

Tactical is Red

TACTICIANS ARE TOOLS TO ACCOMPLISH THE OPERATORS GOAL

Let's start at the bottom: The tactical tier is home to the Red person. Think about electricians for a moment. Before there was the Uniform Building Code in the United States, there were lots of electrical fires. People were doing bad electrical work then, but implementation of the universal standards fixed the competency problem. Today, a master electrician is extremely competent. "How should I do my work?" is no longer the primary question.

A more important one is, "Why do I do my work? What purpose does it serve?"

Imagine the scenario of a builder who has constructed several thousand homes in lifestyle communities during his career so far. He might build 10 homes on one side of a given street and tell an electrician, "Here are 10 homes. Put electricity in them and, oh, by the way, the model home is #5." To a typical, internally and tactically focused person, that extra bit of information would not resonate. What he would take away from that conversation is "I need to put electricity in 10 homes." As a linear thinker, he would most likely start with #1, then #2, and so on.

Why would this be a problem?

A finished model home facilitates the sale of the other houses because future homeowners can tour it and imagine themselves living in the space. The sooner that the potential buyers are able to tour the model home, the quicker the other houses can get sold, even if they are not completed with construction.

Red people, the tacticians, are essential for the support function of an organization, whether doing IT or wiring houses. We need them to be highly competent at what they do. Here's the problem: We also need them to be able to *prioritize* the work. The Red electrician in the example above is not incompetent at installing wiring, but he is incompetent at prioritizing properly. We need the competency of Red people, but it would be beneficial if they would prioritize their work.

In real life, general contractors address this ahead of time by giving the electrician specific instructions: "Do it this way. If you don't do it this way, you don't get paid." That's how prioritization is controlled in the construction industry.

Many IT people are internally, tactically focused. If you are in the technology field, you can probably think of a lot of people who are like this. The challenge is that Red people locate their value in *the work they do* and not the value they achieve. It is as if they are the hammer belonging to a carpenter; they could be used by the carpenter to construct something or to deconstruct something but as long as they take no ownership in the final result, it doesn't even matter what the result is, because they are just a tool. Because they don't connect their work to its value, they feel like they work within a vacuum. As for the leadership, they see tools as easily replaceable.

Let me give you an example of how disconnecting work from value can cause difficulties. Walmart has had an amazing track record of delivering the lowest cost to their customers for over 50 years. Their people are constantly trying to figure out ways to reduce their own cost so they can pass that onto their customers. "Everyday low price" is their value to the market. What if one day, a technologist at Walmart went into work and saw an opportunity to provide a tool that would give Walmart, at least in one area, comparable customer service to a business such as Nordstrom's? Developing and sustaining the tool may cost a considerable amount of the technologist's and potentially other's time, but it would provide better service to their customers. What would Walmart's leaders think of this potential tool? Here is the crux, if it doesn't reduce Walmart's cost or even more importantly their customer's cost, it's really just waste. Customer service is not their value. Technologists will often use their highly competent skills in areas that are not aligned or prioritized to their company's value and therefore not impactful to their organization.

MY PURPOSE IS TO SALE ! LET THE TACTICIANS HANDLE THE TECHNOLOGY

That act may not be as positively perceived by Wal-Mart leadership as you think. Wal-Mart's value proposition is *low-cost*, not necessarily *customer service*. Therefore, you are wasting resources when you spend your time promoting a value which the organization does not prioritize.

You may know a lot about a certain technology, but that is not enough. You must understand what your organization's value proposition is. What benefit does it deliver and to whom?

I used to work for Lockheed Martin running a component of IT infrastructure for the F-22 program. We would see military colonels around all the time, but one day, a general walked in. He asked me, "Son, what do you do?" I replied, "I build military aircraft, sir." He smiled and responded, "You're going to go a long way."

What did he mean? He was saying that *perspective*—how you view what you do—matters a lot. Because I didn't actually build military aircraft. The guy sitting next to me had a PhD in aeronautics from MIT and he didn't build military aircraft, either. The people on the manufacturing floor in Fort Worth, Texas actually built the military aircraft. They are the ones assembling the parts, but I still told the general that I built military aircraft, because my job contributed to that value and that was the ultimate purpose of my job.

What you perceive that you do matters. Even if your job is tactical, you don't work in a vacuum. Do you want to be a leader and an enabler? You need to understand how your role impacts the rest of the organization. Figure out *why* what you do matters. How are you relevant to the people in the lead boat?

"I build military aircraft" was a natural reply for me. If you would never have answered that way, don't lose heart! I believe

MY ROLE: THE ULTIMATE PURPOSE OF MY JOB

this way of thinking can be learned. You can grow to see yourself as an integral part of a larger whole. That's how all Red people deserve to think of themselves.

CIO's / IT DIRECTORS

Operations is Blue

— Strategy (CEO)
— Gen Contractor
— ELECTRICIANS

The people in the operational tier is Blue. Their job is to enable the organization. They are like a general contractor who makes sure the electricians do their job right. Blue people *connect* what the strategist does—which we might call mission or business alignment—with what the operators need to do. Blue people look at the strategist and say, "That's the target? Okay." Then they look at the tactician and say, "Here's the target. To achieve it you need to do xyz." Blue people focus on being enablers.

You can be a Blue person in any role. In fact, I believe that if you are a technology leader, being Blue must be your goal. You must be an enabler because you will not be relevant to your organization before then.

Blue people are the interface between Strategy and Tactics. That means that they are interfacing in two different directions: *toward Strategy*, to enable the business mission, and *toward Tactics*, to direct their job. If you are Blue, you need to mitigate noise and friction while reducing risk. Additionally, you need to work incredibly well cross-functionally, because your job is to enable not only the strategist but also the other people you work with.

If you are an IT leader in the private sector, your goal is to enable the person who runs sales for your region. How do you give them the data they need to be more effective? That strategist may need tools or data or any number of support features. Your job is to get those things from Tactics for Strategy. You enable the organization.

Strategy is Green

The final color is Green, the color of Strategy. The Green person provides direction to the business. As the captain, he controls the rudder: "Turn that way!" Green sets trajectory and vision and culture then gets out of the way.

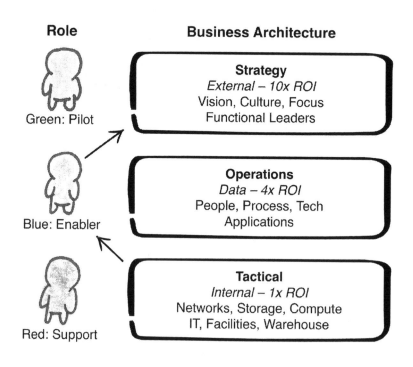

Green people include Chief Executive Officers (CEOs), Chief
Sales Officers (CSOs), Chief Operations Officers (COOs), Managing Directors (MDs), Chief Marketing Officers (CMOs), and others. No matter their title, their job is to provide direction to the organization.

Get in the Boat Whiteboard

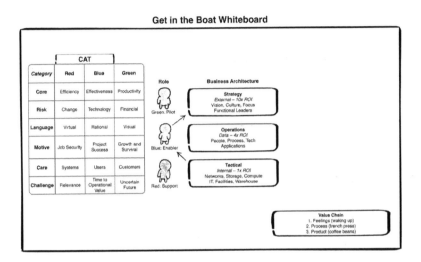

Chapter 5.

Fulfillment in Your Job

In 2007, business speaker and writer Patrick Lencioni published a book called <u>The Three Signs of a Miserable Job</u>, a narrative about a fictional, retired CEO and his quest to be useful. The CEO, Brian Bailey, quickly realizes that a life of retired inactivity is not for him. Instead, he becomes part owner of a small restaurant and tries to turn it around—even if the employees aren't on board. In fact, none of the employees like their jobs. They're miserable.

Anonymity

Throughout the story, Brian discovers the three root causes behind job misery. First, *anonymity*: People are dissatisfied with what they do if they do not know the people with whom they work, especially their supervisor. That's a sign of a miserable job. Back in the 1950s–1970s, MBA professors taught students (who became leaders of many companies today) to distance themselves from people in the workplace. Why? They thought psychological distance would make it easier to fire someone and thus be a more effective leader, able to do what is best for the company without emotional involvement. The problem is that *distance prevents trust.* It raises questions: "Are we in the same tribe? Are we in this together?" The first sign of a miserable job is anonymity.

Immeasurability

The second cause of job misery is *immeasurability*: people, whatever they do, need to be able to achieve many small successes.

Reaching a goal or winning a contest releases testosterone and dopamine to the brain. When we frequently feel successful, our brain's structure changes, making us confident and natural winners.[8]

Likewise, employees need to be measured (or better, to measure themselves) daily for successes. Otherwise, they will not feel fulfilled. Annual reviews fail miserably at this—I'm willing to bet your last annual review actually had little impact on your daily work.

If you are in a commercial, profit-focused organization, the goal is growth in revenue and profitability. The challenge for IT is that, being in a support function, it's often hard to measure your

---

[8] Eugene Sheely, "The Winner Effect: How Success Affects Brain Chemistry," Gamification Co, accessed November 13, 2017. http://www.gamification. co/2014/02/21/the-winner-effect/.

impact on what matters. You can measure internally, but connecting those measurements to what drives the organization is a challenge. IT leaders need to track two or three Key Performance Indicators (KPIs) daily or weekly and update their employees regularly. That way, employees can reach their goals, see their successes, and feel fulfilled. As an example, people who work in sales call centers, a seemingly mundane environment, have always seemed quite happy when I observe them. I attribute this to the immediate feedback they get and the constant incentive contests that are being run.

Irrelevance

The final sign of a miserable job is *irrelevance*. The actions we take are not the most important thing, it's how we impact or positively *enable* other human beings. We must learn how to be relevant. Consider music superstar Taylor Swift or Real Madrid's Cristiano Renaldo. This might catch you off guard, but Taylor's relevance is not due to her voice or song-writing skills nor is Renaldo's relevance due to his footwork abilities on the field. Rather, they are relevant because *they impact other people; namely, their fans.* That is the secret to relevance. What makes you relevant is how you impact other people's lives. Not playing songs, not scoring goals, and not completing successful IT projects—*impact* is the secret.

Sociopaths lack the capability to have empathy for other people, which makes it exceptionally difficult for them to be relevant. You don't often impact people for whom you care nothing about. But unless you're a sociopath, you're wired like all the rest of us and you find relevance in impacting other human beings.

That is how you find fulfillment in work, even within the business architecture we discussed earlier. As you navigate your way among strategists and operators and tacticians, you will gain a relevant and *meaningful* job by impacting others.

Surveying the IT world, I see technology leaders struggling to be relevant with their own senior leaders. The minds of senior leaders are not often like the minds of technology leaders. Senior leaders don't care about the same things technology leaders care about. Technologists must figure out how to impact their functional leaders in a way that they can relate to, which is normally an entirely differently way than the way the technologists would normally think and speak.

Chapter 6.

p.69

CAT: Core

I've created a useful tool that I call the CAT: Care-About Tool. As the name suggests, it identifies what Green and Blue and Red *care about*. We will explore different aspects of the CAT so you can grasp what makes other people tick and learn how to be relevant to them. You become more deeply relevant by identifying and providing what's important to each color.

Red people are internally and tactically focused. They are often highly competent and provide the support for an organization: IT infrastructure, facilities, warehouses. Though Red people sometimes have difficulty prioritizing, they are absolutely needed, whether insourced or outsourced.

Blue people enable the organization by handling operations: people, process, and technology, driven by applications. If Red is the ship's hull, Blue is the engine.

Green people are the functional leaders of our companies, the strategists who provide direction, focus, culture, and vision. They are the captains who set a trajectory for the hull and engine.

Speaking of red and blue, it's an interesting coincidence that I chose those colors to indicate two groups of people who have difficulty communicating, as in the United States, we use those two colors to demarcate the Republican and Democratic parties. Although I did not choose Red and Blue because of that association, thinking about the struggle between the two political parties can be a helpful analogy to understand communication differences. Conservatives and liberals all around the globe struggle to communicate effectively with each other because at their core, *they are speaking a different language.*

Recently I watched a TED Talk given by Megan Phelps-Roper.[9] She is the granddaughter of Fred Phelps, founder of Westboro Baptist Church (WBC), whose members are infamous for protesting at soldiers' funerals carrying signs that read, "Thank God for Dead Soldiers" and using inflammatory language toward just about everyone, such as "God Hates You," and "Thank God for [Hurricane] Katrina." Megan Phelps-Roper grew up in this environment and believed in its ideology. In her TED talk, she shared how the screaming counter-protestors and online attackers did not affect her stance one bit. Head-on confrontation completely failed. She only began to question the WBC ideology when people engaged with her firmly yet lovingly. After months of online and in-person discussions, she completely departed

---

[9]   You can view Megan Phelps-Roper's TED talk on the TED website: https://www.ted.com/talks/megan_phelps_roper_i_grew_up_in_the_westboro_baptist_church_here_s_why_i_left.

from the WBC and now promotes genuine non-hate-filled dialogue.

I doubt the leaders of your organization are anything like the leaders of the WBC. Yet, the principle is universal; to impact someone, you must caringly engage with them without compromising your own convictions.

[handwritten: POLITICS]

What is the core of a conservative? Values that include loyalty, patriotism, fiscal responsibility. What is the core of a liberal? Values that include caring for the weak, equality, social justice. People of different political ideologies often talk past each other because they don't understand one another's core values and reflect them with their language. Are you a conservative trying to communicate with a liberal or are you a liberal trying to communicate with a conservative? You cannot assume your core ideology as the basis for the conversation. You have to frame your perspective in the terms that the other person cares about: connect government's fiscal responsibility to equal opportunity, or social justice to patriotism. Use metaphors and parables. Respect your conversation partner's ideology—not as superior to your own, but as an essential tool for communication. That is the only way political "reds and blues" will be able to dialogue without frustration, confusion, and shouting.

That is also the only way business Reds and Blues and Greens will be able to communicate. Like the political above, these business Colors have a *core*. They have values and assumptions and an ideology they hold dear. To communicate to them, you must know them. As Stephen Covey so wisely said in *The 7 Habits of Highly Effective People*, "Seek first to understand, then to be understood."[10] *Core* is the first element of the Care-About Tool.

---

[10] Stephen R. Covey, *The Seven Habits of Highly Effective People*, 25th Anniversary ed. (New York: Simon & Schuster, 2013), 247.

RED—CORE "EFFICIENCY"

The Core of Red

For Red, the core is *efficiency*. Reds want to do more with less, because in a black-and-white world that inherently makes sense. Why wouldn't you want to do more with less time, less money, less everything? On the surface, it sounds great.

The challenge is that if efficiency does not help the value of your organization, it may be immaterial. Say you're in a health-care organization with revenue of $20 billion. Assuming the IT spend is roughly 8% of revenue, that's $1.6 billion—a significant amount of money. Maybe 20% of that is IT infrastructure, so we're down to $320 million. You're the network communications leader, so your budget is a fraction of that $320 million. Now, I'm an outside vendor, and I tell you that I can save you 2% of your costs. You're thrilled! Saving 2% of a budget (a too-small one, in your view) is very useful. But as you try to get approval for my proposal from higher-ups with greater responsibility—operators like chiefs of medicine, strategists like the CEO—you start to find out that 2% savings in your budget is not necessarily material to Green, nor to the organization. As a Red, your core value of efficiency could blind you from seeing your point of greatest impact to the organization.

BLUE—CORE "EFFECTIVENESS"

The Core of Blue

Effectiveness is the core of Blue. Blue people want to be able to achieve their goals in the most effective way possible. You want to pitch an improvement to the Chief of Medicine. What does he care about? What's his core? *Effectiveness.* He wants more bang for his buck. He doesn't mind paying money to achieve his goal of better patient care. That's not efficiency, by the way—efficiency is spending money to save money. Spending money to get more money is effectiveness. *EFFICIENCY VS EFFECTIVENESS*

So maybe you talk about labor. Help the chief of medicine automate a repetitive task and reduce labor costs, which are probably responsible for 60% of his total costs. Healthcare has many traditionally repetitive tasks that cost time and burn people out. The chief of medicine wants to keep labor around (because high turnover rates are ineffective). Help him accomplish that and you'll be a hero.

For example, nurses have to record patient information and input it into the central system. Traditionally, the nurse would take notes on paper and then later type it into the computer. This caused delays because the nurses had to walk back and forth between patient rooms and the front desk. Today, nurses type information directly into the system using a tablet computer.

The Core of Green

What is material to Green? *Productivity.* When I was the CEO of a services company, I cared about three labor metrics. The first was customer satisfaction. The second was utilization. I wanted my people to be utilized 62–68% of the time. (Utilization higher than 68% was not attainable because the production personnel traveled around the globe.) That percentage was effective, so if someone's utilization was substantially lower, I looked for a root cause. The third metric I cared about was productivity. I took each employee's base cost to the organization, multiplied it by three, and compared it to the revenue that employee produced. If the revenue was over 300% of the total cost, I was happy. That made for a healthy income that we could invest back into the company. As a Green CEO, I loved it when my employees were productive.

Speak to the core

Do you want to communicate more effectively with people at different tiers in your organization? Speak to their core. If you are an IT leader, having provided support in the tactical area for a long time, you'll be tempted to speak to your CEO about efficiency. He'll probably blow you off—efficiency is not his concern. It's core to you, but not to him. Clothe your proposal in something that would matter to him: productivity and growth.

CEO's

Remember "measure what matters"? Efficiency is a measure of what matters for you. But the CEO is measured on *growth*. Unless you help him improve what he is measured on, you will remain irrelevant. The organization's value proposition is the same for both of you and you are striving toward the same overarching goal, but your individual contributions are distinct and your measurements are unique.

To impact others and be relevant you must understand the core of Red, the core of Blue, and the core of Green. In short:

- Red – Efficiency – *SPENDING MONEY TO SAVE MONEY*
- Blue – Effectiveness – *SPENDING MONEY TO GET MORE MONEY*
- Green – Productivity – *CUSTOMER SAT / UTILIZATION) PRODUCTIVITY*

WHAT ARE MY CUSTOMERS MEASURED ON?

Let's take an example from the food industry. Blue people are focused on process and components associated with that process, like key performance indicators (KPIs). One of the by-product of the food industry is waste and food manufacturers spend a lot of time reducing waste. Waste is sometimes quite disgusting (especially if you know what the food industry is doing with some of the waste). The nicest example from the food industry may be cookie ice cream.

One large food company was producing cookies at one end of their plant and ice cream on the other end. As always, their processes produced waste. What does waste from cookies look like? Cookie crumbs!

For hundreds of years, people have been reusing food waste for food production. What to do with stale bread? Make croutons or use it in recipes such as bread pudding or ribollita. What did owners of small farms feed their pigs? They fed them leftovers, food waste. Then, in due time, the pigs become food themselves. That was traditionally what was done hundreds of years ago and it's still happening today. _EFFICIENT_

The ice cream example is similar. The Blue people who were running the production process in the cookie factory asked themselves, "How can we reduce waste?" They came up with an idea: Reuse it by putting it into ice cream. Putting cookie crumbs into ice cream reuses waste, thus making the factory more efficient at producing cookies.

Now cookie ice cream was on the market. And then something unforeseen happened: People didn't just like it, they loved the cookie ice cream! The factories increased production and used up every last bit of cookie waste (i.e. crumbs) for cookie ice cream. But consumers still wanted to buy more, so the company had to come up with something new.

Maybe you've seen their new idea in your local supermarket. Now there is not only cookie ice cream with crumbs inside, but also cookie ice cream with whole cookies inside! Breaking whole cookies just for the sake of ice cream doesn't make sense. Why not put the full cookies into the ice cream to address customer demand? That's what the companies have done.

Efficiency means completing a process with minimum waste. Productivity means creating value. Happily, like cookie ice cream, sometimes you can have both!

Chapter 7.

p. 69
CAT: Risk

What is the greatest risk for Red, for Blue, and for Green?

We all have personal risk: You can't drive your car to work without risking an accident, however unlikely. In the same way, other forms of risk are present in business. Take financial risk, for instance; a business may have insufficient capital to fund its projects, or feel squeezed by debt service payments, or lack cash flow. Technology comes with risks, too: the risk of systems crashing, the risk of outages to essential applications. Compliance risk affects banking, healthcare, and financial services companies, among others. Regulations are heavy worldwide, with severe penalties for noncompliance. Change—inside or outside the business—is risky too. "The way things have always been" seems safe…at least until stagnancy and immobility turn you into a dinosaur.

Which Colors care about which risks?

- Red people primarily deal with the risk of change. Their job is to update networks and replace outdated systems and every time they try something new they invite the risk of disaster.

- Blue people focus on operational risk. Are the key processes working? Is the customer satisfied?

- Green people worry about financial risk every day. Their goal is productivity and profitability, so they handle the business numbers.

Productivity
& profitability

- Together, Blue and Green deal with compliance risk. Blue oversees the tools that must comply, while Green is held responsible for any noncompliance.

Risk matters. Business leaders decide on courses of action based on their perception of threats to the business. Thus, when you speak to Blue or Green, remember what they are worrying about and help allay their fears.

A friend of Robert Schaffner shared the following story with him:

He was at dinner with two friends, the first a sales trainer, and the second a solar panel salesman to homeowners. He asked the second friend, "How's business?"

"Really hard. Solar panels are being shipped in from China and driving prices down. The technology is becoming mainstream and lots of other solar panel companies are starting up."

They talked about what he could do to improve his business. The sales trainer friend asked, "What risks are associated with installing solar panels?"

"There aren't really any risks. The vendors guarantee the solar panels for a certain number of years. If a panel breaks, you can get it replaced."

Then they thought of this question: How easy is it to uninstall solar panels?

The answer was: It's really easy and very fast. You drive up with a truck; you set up the ladder; you get on the roof; you start to uninstall them. Half an hour later, you have a whole load of solar panels in your truck.

The friends came up with the idea of manual protection for solar panels, where they need a special tool to uninstall them. The tool itself doesn't cost much, but without it, other tools cannot be used to uninstall solar panels. If someone comes by and wants to steal the panels, they will need half an hour to break the solar panel lock. The required effort is much higher.

The solar panel salesman began having conversations with his customers. He would say, "Congratulations on purchasing solar panels. Installing panels on your roof is a major investment and while they will pay for themselves over time, that will take a few years. In the meantime, do you take vacations? Do you travel for business? Does your house ever sit empty for a few days?" The answer is normally, "Yes, of course."

"Well, did you know that uninstalling panels is not that hard? But we have a solution that locks the solar panels in place and makes it harder to uninstall them. That will help prevent people from dropping by and stealing them. Of course, this is an optional item and you don't need to purchase it. But I thought you might want to consider it."

After introducing this offer, the friend's business picked up quite dramatically. Not everyone purchased the manual lock, *but many did. He had thought deeply about the end customer's potential risks and invented a solution before they even knew they had a problem.*

Half a year later, everyone in the industry offered a similar feature. The competitive advantage was gone, which was a disappointment — but my friend had gotten to spur an industry change. Today, most every solar panel installation requires special tools to uninstall.

The solar panel salesman gained a competitive advantage by recognizing a risk facing end customers and offering a timely solution. The lesson here does not just apply to salespeople, it applies to all of us who have to "sell" something internally. Make clear that you understand the specific risks of the person you are selling to. Speak to those risks and offer solutions. That makes your offer much more relevant.

KNOW THE CUSTOMER

Chapter 8.

p. 69 CAT: Language

While earlier generations may not have ventured far from their hometown, travel, including international travel, is becoming more common and accessible to the average person in this modern age. Air travel is no longer just for the elite. Americans, especially, for the first time in their lives are visiting places where they are the non-dominant culture. How they navigate their experience will make the difference on how they perceive their journey. Do they learn key phrases in the language of the country? Have they researched basic customs and culture?

In the United States, it's common for someone to casually ask a stranger that one has struck up a conversation with, "So, what do you do for a living?" as it is considered taking an interest in that person's life and his day to day activities. In some other countries, it would be considered prying or elitist to ask a stranger that question, or even a casual acquaintance, in the same way that it would be intrusive to ask someone how much income they earned last year.

Even when people appear to speak the same language, things can get tricky. One British woman related a story to me from her early days of living in California:

> *When I was in my 20s during the late 1970s, my husband and I had recently moved from England to California and we invited another young couple over for dinner after church one Sunday.*
>
> *"What are we having?" our new friends asked after they arrived and we were sitting in the living room together.*
>
> *"Oh," I replied, lightly, "I thought we'd have a nice joint."*
>
> *The couple's faces were absolutely aghast.*
>
> *My husband immediately understood the language mishap. "She means roast beef! She means the meat!"*

Language is a tricky thing. Our challenge is that we get caught in two areas. First, we get caught in the *details*. Imagine you are looking at a tree in a forest. Ignoring the surrounding trees (the big picture) is problematic. Tunnel vision limits your broader view of the obstacles ahead. You may be very skillful at tending your tree, which provides you with confidence in this complex world. But many outside factors are impacting your tree. What if there's a fire burning nearby? If you don't dig a ditch, you can care for the tree all you want, but it will soon be consumed by fire. That problem arises when you go from macro to micro too quickly. IT people often go deep into the minutiae of a subject before understanding it as a whole.

The second challenge is that we get caught in *jargon*. I think IT uses the most jargon of any industry apart from military and healthcare. For example, "Our pen-tester is finally finished with the bloatware—it showed quite some code smell after some brute force." (If you didn't understand that sentence, don't worry. It's not your fault. And if you did understand the sentence, promise me never to say anything like it!)

Why do we speak in jargon? Because it's useful to speed up communication. You want to say something quickly, so you turn it into an acronym. But most people in the organization outside of the IT department do not share this lexicon. Using jargon while trying to communicate with them becomes a problem. Sometimes, jargon has become so natural and second-nature to us that we aren't even aware that we are using it.

Take the word "virtualization," for instance. Everyone in IT uses that word. It's a very Red word; you won't hear a Blue or Green person talking that way. Red uses *virtual* language.

My mother is in her 80s. She has been a homemaker most of her life, and her passions are growing beautiful flowers and canning delicious preserves. If I went home to my mother and said, "Hey mom, can we talk about virtualization?" that would be a very short conversation. She'd probably reply bluntly, in her no-nonsense manner, "No. I don't know what that means, so I don't really want to talk about it." That's what Blue and Green people would like to say, too.

Our jargon does not resonate outside of our protective space. Moreover, it makes us irrelevant. We need to understand that people use different words. What is virtualization? It's the ability to take multiple computer nodes and put them on one physical node, therefore attaining better efficiency of the computer nodes. There used to be many under-utilized resources inside computers, but virtualization eliminates that. It also gives you a centralized view of your computing capacity. That's what we mean by virtualization.

Blue people use *rational* language. In the application-based Blue world, collapsing multiple applications into one business project is called "rationalization". Rationalization is similar to virtualization in the Red world, so you could use it as a synonym.

Green strategists use *visual* language. They want visibility into their environment, so we can use the word "digitalization" or "visualization" for them. This is somewhat of a paraphrase rather than a direct translation. That said, I would definitely not use the word "virtualization" with someone who is a CEO. That would not connect with his core. I would tell him, "We want to digitize so that we can visualize our environment more effectively." That would resonate. It would even resonate with my mom: "Mom, can you visualize a bed of flowers outside your window?" I'm sure she could.

VIRTUALIZATION   RATIONALIZATION   VISUALISATION

Chapter 9.

CAT: Motivation, Care, and Challenge

In addition to the core of who they are, the risks that impact them, and the language they use, the colors have different core motivations.

Motivation

My estimation, after many years in the IT world, is that the core motivator for Red is job security. Technologists are trying constantly to protect our jobs. That might seem obvious: we have bills to pay and may have families to feed, clothe, and shelter, as well. But as you communicate to people higher up the architectural level, you will find that, though they all care about job security, it is not their principal motivator. Attempting to motivate them with *your* principal motivator leads to irrelevance.

Blue cares a lot about **time**: time to market, time to operational value, time to everything. Why does Blue care about time? Because it affects their key motivator, *project success*. Blues need to be successful at their projects, whereas a Red person in that same project may care about an element of it but not the entire project. Blue has more of a macro view; Red, a micro view.

To be a business enabler, you must be able to reach from Blue down to Red so that they can support your project. And you need to reach up to Green to obtain their protection and funding so you can be successful in your project. Green's principal value is **growth**. In commercially-focused organizations, growth is revenue and profitability. The other side of that coin is **survival**. Not survival in the sense of job security, but at the very macro level: survival of the organization itself.

Care

Because of those principal motivations, what each color cares about is different. The Red person cares about the element itself; in the information technology world, we would call that a system. Red cares about routers and servers and code.

Blue cares not about the system, but about the **processes** that use the system. Blue also cares about the people who need the system—the **users**.

Green owns the business model. The business model defines the go-to market and is the basis for the overall customer journey. Thus, Green cares most about the organization's **customer** or consumer. In healthcare, that would be the patient or the physician. For banking, it's the commercial or the retail client.

Challenge

If you think about business as a 400-metre hurdles race, each color faces a different type of hurdle:

Green is confronted by an **uncertain future**. If you are trying to talk to Green people, focus on uncertainty, because that's their challenge. Companies are vying for supremacy, markets are changing, industries are undergoing transformation, and consumer preferences are developing. These pressures create uncertainty and Green leaders spend most of their time responding to that uncertainty.

Blue's challenge is achieving value in business projects as quickly as possible: **time to operational value.**

Red people face the challenge of **relevance**. How do we impact other people's lives? How do technologists use their tactical role to impact the enablers, or to become the enablers? The answer is that they must positively aid their organization.

These challenges are the most important cultural distinction between Red, Blue, and Green. Understand what your coworkers throughout the organization are facing. Their everyday concerns may not be yours and that's okay. Seek to view the world through their eyes for a moment, then speak from that perspective.

CAT

Category	Red	Blue	Green
Core	Efficiency	Effectiveness	Productivity
Risk	Change	Technology	Financial
Language	Virtual	Rational	Visual
Motive	Job Security	*TIME* Project Success	Growth and Survival *↳BUSINESS MATURITY*
Care	Systems	*Processes* Users	Customers
Challenge	Relevance	Time to Operational Value	Uncertain Future

Get in the Boat Whiteboard

SECTION III.

UNDERSTAND GREEN

Chapter 10.

Business Model Canvas
VALUE PROPOSITION

LEGO

Back in 2003, LEGO was the eighth-largest toy company in the world. They had been around for just over 75 years making plastic bricks for kids, but they were on the brink of collapse. They had been a worldwide favorite of children for many years but because of their strategic decisions in the late 1990s, they were forced to reevaluate.

What went wrong? Well, they listened to every management theorist in the world on how to innovate and they did it all. LEGO had diversified into video games and theme parks, but in so doing had overextended itself. The Green people who were responsible for creating LEGO's vision and culture had failed at their job. An organization can't typically address many new markets with many new products; LEGO certainly couldn't, anyway.

Jørgen Vig Knudstorp, who became their CEO in 2003, realized that LEGO had lost its way; they had forgotten why it existed. It is critical to a global organization that it has an understanding of why it exists and to focus solely on that value. This reason is called a value proposition; it is the why, it is the purpose. After some self-reflection, LEGO came up with their value, which was "to teach children problem solving skills, which is a critical 21st century skill."[11] That is what they were missing! Problem-solving skills is the goal; therefore, LEGO sets should contain parts and pieces that force children to think about how to put stuff together. Now LEGO's products are aimed at a single value proposition: We teach children problem solving skills.

Why THE B2 EXIST

How is LEGO doing today? It's a juggernaut. LEGO is the second-largest toy company, and—based on blocks—the largest construction company in the world. It produces 15 billion blocks a year. They don't just sell toys, they have encouraged buy-in from educational systems who offer things such as LEGO Robotic Camps and LEGO Engineering Camps. There are regional LEGO Leagues which have robotic competitions for children. Plus, the LEGO Batman movie came out in February 2017,

---

[11] https://hbr.org/2009/01/lego-ceo-jorgen-vig-knudstorp-on-leading-through-survival-and-growth

commended by critics, loved by fans, and hailed by some as one of the best Batman movies ever. LEGO today is an incredibly successful company because it recovered its *why, its purpose, its value proposition*. Today, due to a very focused value proposition and thousands of Blue people that execute that strategy each day, LEGO has become a breakaway success after just 90 years!

We in IT often focus on the building blocks of our jobs, the specifics of what we do. But that commoditizes our work. The company could outsource your job and get the same building blocks done. See, hooking up a network is of no value to your company until you explicitly connect it to the value proposition. You can't think only about LEGOS. You must connect the dots between what you do and what the company needs. Your leadership doesn't buy what you do—they buy why you do it. That's why they pay you: because you help them achieve the *why*.

Business theorist and consultant Alexander Osterwalder wrote the book Business Model Generation: A Handbook for Visionaries, Game Changers, and Challengers, which explains how the various aspects of your business fit together into a whole. Green strategists think about this big picture regularly, because Green is in charge of strategy. Red never thinks about the big picture, as Red is too busy delving into a single component. Blue does not naturally live in the realm of the business model but *understands it* and *can use it* to connect with Green. To connect with Green, you must speak the Green language—and the Green language is all about the business model.

I like Osterwalder's work, but have changed some elements to make it better fit this context. Here's my modified version of the Business Model Canvas.

GREEN SPEAKS THIS LANGUAGE

• USE THESE TYPE TERMS @ MEETING

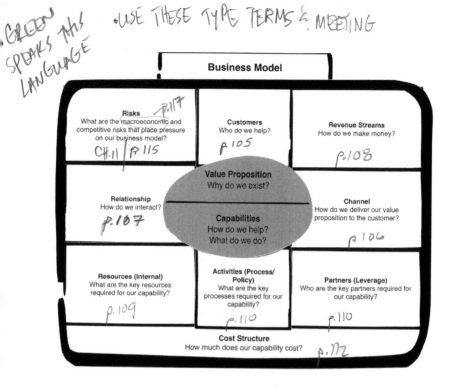

Business Model

Risks *p.117* What are the macroeconomic and competitive risks that place pressure on our business model? *CH.11 / p 115*	Customers Who do we help? *p 105*	Revenue Streams How do we make money? *p.108*
Relationship How do we interact? *p.107*	Value Proposition Why do we exist? Capabilities How do we help? What do we do?	Channel How do we deliver our value proposition to the customer? *p 106*
Resources (Internal) What are the key resources required for our capability? *p.109*	Activities (Process/Policy) What are the key processes required for our capability? *p.110*	Partners (Leverage) Who are the key partners required for our capability? *p.110*

Cost Structure
How much does our capability cost? *p.112*

Value proposition

Beginning at the center, the initial point in any business model is your value proposition. What can you promise and deliver to the customer? Here are some potential elements of your value proposition:

- Newness – we offer the newest way of doing XYZ; e.g., new and improve dishwasher soap

- Performance – we are the best at the task; e.g., the fastest PC

- Customization – we will customize our system to fit your precise needs; e.g., a custom suit

- Dependability – we will get the job done reliably; e.g., Rolls Royce engines have a hundred-year track record of excellence

- Design – our product looks better than our competitors' products; e.g., the original Apple iPhone vs. other smartphones at that time

- Brand – our name adds value to our product; e.g., Rolex, Harley-Davidson

- Price – we are the cheapest option; e.g., EasyJet in Europe, on which airline I once flew my family of five from London to Rome for $200 total

- Cost reduction – we are cheaper than your current way of doing things; e.g., Software as a service (SaaS) has decreased the large amount of money I used to spend on traditional application software

- Guarantee – we reduce your risk in buying from us; e.g., Nordstrom's guarantee – if you don't like it you can return it, no matter what

- Skill acquisition – we teach you how to do something; e.g., LEGO teaches children problem-solving skills

Here are some possible value propositions.

- Healthcare: "We have top-rate physicians who deliver treatments in a multitude of specialties with access to specialized equipment (proton therapy machines, etc.) that provide the best possible patient care." (Reduced Risk and Top Performance)

- Property Management: "We are the largest real estate services firm in the world with over five million square feet of property under management in over 100 countries.

Our 70,000 employees in 400 global offices have the expertise to provide all of your commercial real estate needs." (Reduced Risk, Cost Reduction, Dependability, and Brand)

- Pharmaceutical: "Improving the quality of life through research driven initiatives that deliver critically needed therapies for the global health community. (Newness and Design)

- Consumer Data Source: "We are the leading source of critical information so customer can make better decisions." (Reduce Risk and Reduced Cost)

- Specialty Store (Hardware): "We provide the widest product selection coupled with our team's expert knowhow that allow our customer's home renovations to be successful every time." (Risk Reduction, Cost Reduction, Price, and Brand)

Your organization's value proposition likely includes one or more of those elements. Can you grab a piece of paper and write it down, right now? If not, you need to search it out. Maybe you have been working with your product for so long you've forgotten what it is for. You might find it hard to express just what it is that your organization does.

If you work for a US publicly-traded company that must comply with Securities and Exchange Commission (SEC) regulations, look for the value proposition inside your company's Form 10-K. (A Form 10-K is an annual report required by the United States SEC that gives a comprehensive summary of a company's financial performance.) Section 1 or Item 1 explains what the business offers—the value proposition. For example, look at the first page of Coca-Cola's 10-K, linked to in the footnote of this sentence.[12]

If you're in a private company, check out your large competitors. Any of them who are public must submit a Form 10-K, and you can find their value proposition as a starting point for your own. Also look up your own organization's annual report, as that may contain a statement of your value proposition. If your organization is held publicly in one of the global exchanges, London Stock Exchange, Euronext, Japan Exchange, etc., they will need to comply with security regulations in those countries and submit to standard reporting. Most annual reports will disclose the nature of your company's business and provide important insight.

Another way to gather this understanding is to talk to your company salespeople. Ask them, "What do our customers like about us? Why do they buy from us?" Salespeople have to communicate the organization's value every day.

What you read in the 10-K or hear from the salespeople may be a generic value proposition that your competitors could use too. You should narrow it down so that it is specific to your company. Go back to the salespeople and say, "I read such-and-such in our competitor's 10-K. How do we respond to that? Why are we still a better choice?" Those questions will further define the unique value you offer.

Now, if you work for a very large company like Berkshire Hathaway—a conglomerate—you want to work out the business model for the division you work for. Berkshire Hathaway owns GEICO, BNSF Railway, and Pampered Chef. You can bet those

---

[12] The Coca-Cola Company, "2016 Annual Report on Form 10-K," The Coca-Cola Company, accessed November 13, 2017. http://www.coca-colacompany.com/content/dam/journey/us/en/private/fileassets/pdf/investors/2016-AR-10-K.pdf.

three have quite distinct business models. If you work for GE-ICO, the business model for all of Berkshire Hathaway will be much less applicable to you than the business model of GEICO alone.

Most technologists work in organizations whose value proposition does not include technology. Coca-Cola has over 100,000 employees, many of whom fill tactical roles—but its value proposition has everything to do with drinks and nothing to do with technology. BNSF railroad needs technologists, but offers rail transportation. Are you in a situation like this? You work in the background, providing tactical support. Knowing the organization's value to its average customer is especially important for you. Understand that you do contribute to that value, just a few steps removed. To communicate with Green, you need to talk in the context of the value proposition.

The business core

At the core of the value of any business is this question of purpose. What is our meaning? Why do we exist? These are really questions about value. And the question of value at the level of strategy determines the behavior of the business at the level of operations and at the level of tactics.

- at the level of operations: *How do we act?*

- at the level of tactics: *What do we do?*

Simon Sinek, a marketing author and speaker touches on this concept of why you exist through his very popular TED talk on how great leaders "start with why."[13]

---

[13] You can view Simon Sinek's TED talk on the TED website: https://www.ted.com/talks/simon_sinek_how_great_leaders_inspire_action.

Ask most people about their job and they tell you their job title or tell you a general account of what they do. "I am a kindergarten teacher," or "I am a software engineer," or "I am a manager". For instance, say it's 1997 and I work for Hewlett-Packard: I'll tell you, "I make computers." Ask Steve Jobs in 1997 what he does, and he'll say, "I think different."

That "Think Different" slogan traces back to the early 1980s, when IBM used the slogan "THINK." Jobs hijacked that slogan, using it in that famous "1984" Super Bowl commercial. The point was, "We at Apple are people who think differently. Are you that kind of person? Then you'll want to buy what we make." That's not a typical sales message. Normally you hear, "Here's what we have on the shelf." Apple said, "Here's *why* we have anything on the shelf at all."

Apple is successful in part because it starts with why. Back in 1997, HP was a more successful company; Apple was on the verge of collapse. But Steve Jobs returned and helped Apple find its way again. Apple released the iMac in 1997, the iPod in 2001, the iPhone in 2007, and the iPad in 2008. Today in 2017, they closed last fiscal year at $217 billion in revenue, almost 25% net income. Apple is the strongest company that has ever existed and that is not solely because of what it has done. It's because Apple has focused on *why* it does what it does.

PRESIDIO - WE PROVIDE DIGITAL TRANSFORMATION PRODUCTS
& PROFESSIONAL
SERVICES.

Customer

Your value proposition and your customer are tied together. If you work at LEGO, your value proposition is "We teach children problem-solving skills." Only certain people care about that.

Who are those people? Parents, grandparents, educators, and others who care about minds of children ages 3–12. That is the heart of your consumer base and you need to know that before you start building out the rest of your business model.

Within the broad category of *customers* are multiple groups. Market segmentation places customers into these groups, which are often called "niche markets." For instance, a bank offers its services both to individuals and to retail clients.

After first determining your value proposition and then identifying your customer, you can transition to channel and relationship. Your customer's identity determines the channel and relationship that will be most effective; thus, channel and relationship come right after it. In short, channel deals with the *creation* of a bond with the customer, and relationship deals with *sustaining* that bond.

Channel

A channel is a "means employed to distribute goods or services from producers to consumers."[14] So, your channel is how you deliver your value proposition to your customer.

Channels are commonly divided into *direct* and *indirect* channels. A direct channel is one that your company owns; a sales force, for example, or your website's e-commerce platform. Amazon sells most of its wares through a direct channel: Amazon.

---

[14] BusinessDictionary.com, "Channel," WebFinance, Inc., accessed November 13, 2017. http://www.businessdictionary.com/definition/channel.html.

com. Apple sells many devices through its own stores, another direct channel.

Apple also partners with companies like Best Buy to sell its devices in Best Buy's stores. This is an indirect channel, because Apple does not own Best Buy. In Europe, where Apple has few stores, it uses this "partner model" or "affiliate model" extensively. Wholesalers, intermediaries, and resellers all belong to an indirect channel.

How your organization gets to market impacts how your organization creates value. To be relevant, you must understand channels.

Relationship

The relationship is the sustaining part. How do you want to interact to sustain a relationship with your clients?

In banking today, the relationship between younger clients and their bank is primarily online. The channel is an online portal. How do banks sustain that relationship? With accessible ATMs everywhere so the young people can easily access their money.

You can see how this affects a bank's business model. A single branch location costs multiple millions of dollars while many young people would be just as happy with an ATM. The bank might not be able to do away with branches entirely, but it could adjust its ratio of branches to ATMs.

Customer support call centers are another kind of relationship-sustainer. When you have trouble with the company's product you call customer support and, hopefully, get off the phone happy.

The relationship that apps like Dropbox sustain is largely self-service, with email or phone support as a backup.

You want to sustain the relationship with the customer for long-term partnership and mutual profitability.

- Let's summarize thus far with LEGO's business model.
- Value proposition: We teach children problem-solving skills
- Customers: Parents of children ages 3–12
- Channel: Online; retailers
- Relationship: theme parks, video games, movies, packaging, camps

Revenue streams

Value proposition, customer, channel, and relationship work together to create *revenue streams* in a commercial-based model.

Two common types of revenue streams are transactional and recurring. Historically, in IT infrastructure, we sold devices transactionally. A company would purchase infrastructure for their computer environment for the next three to five years. It was a large capital spend up front, then very little for the next few years. That's called transactional selling. Today, most businesses are looking for a recurring monthly revenue stream. They may

rent equipment instead of selling it, or offer monthly maintenance plans.

Figure out which revenue streams your company has so that
you can tie your work into them. In a commercial company, the
question that you are trying to figure out is, "How does our organization make money?" Because if you can tie what you do into
how your organization makes money, that makes you valuable.

Capability

Your capabilities support your value proposition—the "how" and
"what" to your "why". For LEGO, the capability of plastic blocks
supports its value proposition of teaching problem-solving skills.

Capability component #1: Resources (internal)

Capabilities are built from three components, the first of which
is the internal resources of your organization: intellectual capital,
brick and mortar, human resources, financial capital, political
capital. Here are some resources a hospital might have:

- People (administration, nurses, physicians)

- Equipment (MRI machines, beds, stethoscopes)

- Financial capital (debt, endowments)

- Political capital (community involvement, relationships
  with lawmakers)

Capability component #2: Partners (leverage) (External)

You also need external resources. These resources are owned not by you but by another company. Why would you use others' resources instead of acquiring your own? Because you want to leverage others' expertise and equipment. Instead of expending resources to reach expert status, partner with the expert.

Technology companies may partner with a data analytics provider, a multiple development provider, a digitalization provider. Healthcare companies partner with labs, insurers, app providers for Electronic Medical Records software, equipment provides like Siemens, food service partners for the cafeteria.

BOLD Capability component #3: Activities (process and policy) *people* *partners*

We must integrate these internal resources and external resources into an ongoing production model. Doing business ad hoc slows the process down because it demands thought every time. Instead, we must set up *activities*—what we might call processes or policies.

Consider the mission-based organization of a police force. One policy is that when the 911 operator dispatches officers, their body cameras turn on. That policy should quickly become routine, such that in every critical situation the higher-ups have visibility even if they are not on site.

I ask many of my speaking audiences how many applications and how many processes the average business has. Generally, they think a business has *few* applications and *many* processes. The problem is that they're confusing process and procedures.

See, there are only a few processes in any given business. Here are some of the processes of a healthcare organization:

EACH DEPARTMENT HAS A PROCESS

Processes

- Admissions
- Discharge
- Housekeeping
- Scheduling
- Data analysis
- Point of care
- Training

SALES

So, to create a capability, you need internal resources and external resources (partners) and activities: processes and policies that enable you to carry out a task repeatedly and sustainably.

Packaging

Everything above the centerline of the Business Model Canvas drives the value proposition. Everything beneath the line drives capabilities. *Packaging* is how you present the combination of the value proposition and the capability. For instance, one could express the iPhone's value proposition as "One device that does everything." The capability is the product, the phone, that fulfills the promise.

Packaging refers, literally, to the box that the iPhone comes in. That is the physical, tangible presentation of the product to the customer. However, packaging is also *conceptual.* Apple "packages" its value proposition and capability together by clearly explaining them to prospects via its website and advertising.[15] Prospects who find the packaging easy to digest are more likely to

---

[15]   https://www.networkworld.com/article/2221536/data-center/inside-apple-s-secret-packaging-room.html

purchase the product. So, packaging is how you present a product or service, both physically and conceptually.

How well you package value proposition and capability together affects your margins. Have you ever opened an Apple product? It's like Christmas! Opening the iPhone box is exciting in and of itself. In fact, to "ensure that opening the box is a unique experience, Apple employs a designer whose sole job is packaging. The company also has a designer…devoted to opening hundreds of prototype boxes. That designer creates and tests endless versions of box shape, angles and tapes."[16]

Packaging reinforces brand and is one reason the customer can choose you over competitors. Packaging your value proposition and capability excellently will increase your gross margin.

Cost ⟶EXPENSES [I PAY TO RUN THE BUSINESS]

Of course, delivering your capabilities costs you something. These costs may be fixed, like renting a facility, or variable, like using more electricity for an extra production run. Costs offset revenue, and in a commercial company, the difference between the two is profitability.

Summary

Why think about business models? Because thinking this way helps you tie what you do into what your business needs. Technologists are often treated like short-order cooks: "Do this" and "Do that" with no sense of direction. They are given orders to do

---

[16] "How Packaging Gives Apple's Buyers a Sensory Experience that Reinforces Brand," Personalics, accessed November 13, 2017. https://www.personalics.com/2016/02/03/sensory-design-packaging/.

certain tasks but not told how they are relevant to the business. To become relevant, technologists must get ahead of the game and figure out *why* people are "ordering" such-and-such. Then, being informed, the technologist can deliver the right solution—maybe even a better one than they were asked for. That is how the business model ties into Michael Porter's value chain: the business model helps you connect Red support to Blue enablement to Green strategy.

BUSINESS MODEL
P. 100

Chapter 11.

Risk

Risk substantially impacts the business model. If technologists are to be relevant enablers, they must grasp the perceived risks that leadership deals with daily. I have spent time in many business environments and it has been my observation that most technology leaders do not truly understand the risks of their own businesses. Why? Because technologists dwell in a place removed from other business people. The technologist only sees the macro-economic or competitive risk from an internal viewpoint, therefore many times those risk don't resonate with them since it's not directly impacting them. Technologists struggle to comprehend and empathize these risks.

To learn about risk, let's return to the Form 10-K. Earlier, we found the value proposition in Section 1. Risks are enumerated after that section in Section or Item 1a. Here are a few of the risks Coca-Cola lists on its 10-K (page 10).

- "Obesity and other health-related concerns may reduce demand for some of our products.

- Water scarcity and poor quality could negatively impact the Coca-Cola system's costs and capacity.

- If we do not address evolving consumer preferences, our business could suffer.

- Increased competition and capabilities in the marketplace could hurt our business.

- If we are not successful in our innovation activities, our financial results may be negatively affected.

- We rely on our bottling partners for a significant portion of our business. If we are unable to maintain good relationships with our bottling partners, our business could suffer."[17]

Once you know the risks your leadership is worried about, you can become relevant simply by *connecting your current projects to those risks*. Are you trying to copy a feature your competitor beat you to? That's competitive risk. Are you developing a new product you think the market will love? Innovation risk. Are you customizing a program to please a client? Relationship risk. I'll bet you can connect your most significant projects to business risks quite easily. Then, next time you talk with a Green leader, share how much time you've spent this past month reducing the risk the business faces. To be relevant, attach the projects you work on to risks associated with your business.

---

[17] Coca-Cola Company, "Form 10-K."

Data collection and mind mapping

The need to attach projects to risks systematically demands a new data collection methodology. I recommend *mind mapping*. If you've never used mind mapping before, think about a pad of sticky notes. You take every piece of information you know about a given subject, put each one on a separate note, and place it onto a whiteboard. Next, you organize the notes by perceiving patterns and grouping related notes into categories. Finally, you step back and visually apprehend the whole topic.

Mind mapping can also be done digitally. (Save the trees!) The program I use is XMind, which has a very shallow learning curve. You can become adept at it in about half an hour. It's available for both Windows and Mac, and—best of all—the basic version is free![18] *RESEARCH!*

Now you can write and post your sticky notes electronically. Collect and collate data. You'll begin to notice connections—like connections between the work you do every day and the business risks Green strategists can't stop thinking about.

←OUTSIDE WORLD/EXTERNAL RISK

Macroeconomic risk: PESTLE

PESTLE is a helpful tool for analyzing the microeconomic and macroeconomic risks threatening your organization. Originally known as PEST, this tool has in more recent years been given an L and final E to represent additional risks. It categorizes risks associated with an organization so that stakeholders can systematically identify future obstacles.

The beauty of using PESTLE to analyze the outside world is that it forces you to start thinking Green. It helps you develop

---

[18] You can download the program on XMind's website: https://www.xmind.net.

questions that resonate with Green people. While simple, it's extremely effective and powerful.

PESTLE is an acronym, standing for **P**olitical, **E**conomic, **S**ocial, **T**echnology, **L**egal, and **E**cological. Here are some examples of risks within each category.[19]

Political

* Government stability
* Freedom of speech, corruption, party in control
* Regulation trends
* Tax policy, and trade controls
* War
* Government policy
* Elections
* Terrorism
* Likely changes to the political environment

Economic

* Stage of business cycle
* Current and projected economic growth
* International trends
* Job growth
* Inflation and interest rates
* Unemployment and labor supply

---

[19] These examples are drawn from the article "What Are the Driving Forces of PESTLE Analysis?," ToughNickel, accessed November 13, 2017. https://toughnickel.com/business/What-is-PESTLE-analysis.

- Levels of disposable income across economy and income distribution
- Globalization
- Likely changes to the economic environment

Social

- Population growth and demographics
- Health, education, and social mobility of the population
- Consumer attitudes
- Advertising and media
- National and regional culture
- Lifestyle choices and attitudes to these
- Levels of health and education
- Major events
- Socio-cultural changes

Technological

- Impact of new technologies
- Inventions and innovations
- The internet and how it affects working and business
- Licensing and patents
- Research funding and development

Legal

- Home legislation
- International legislation

- Employment law
- New laws
- Regulatory bodies
- Environmental regulation
- Industry-specific regulations
- Consumer protection

Ecological

- Ecology
- International environmental issues
- National environmental issues
- Local environmental issues
- Environmental regulations

[handwritten: WHAT RISK DUES MY CLIENT FACE?]

In summary, to understand Green, you must grasp how your business works on the macro level. You must connect your projects to the specific risks your business is facing. How? By collecting data and organizing it through mind mapping. PESTLE is a tool that helps you identify risks your business is facing. After you identify the risk for Green, share with your business leaders how you can help mitigate their risk.

Once you have some experience using PESTLE, you can use it on the fly in conversations. Listen to what the Green strategist is saying, gather data from his words, and connect that data to risks. Ask questions to make latent risks visible and active. Then, offer a solution: "It sounds like you're dealing with major political risk. We might be able to resolve that by…." The goal of mind mapping and thinking through PESTLE is recognizing risks to

[handwritten: LISTEN, UNDERSTAND, & PROVIDE A SOLUTION]

the Green strategies and helping enable them to mitigate those risks. Every risk is a growth opportunity.

Competitive risk: Porter's Five Forces

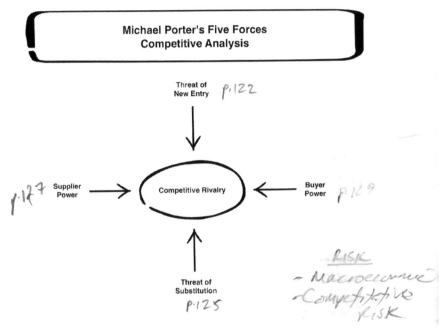

Michael Porter's Five Forces
Competitive Analysis

Threat of New Entry *p.122*

Supplier Power *p.117* → Competitive Rivalry ← Buyer Power *p.129*

Threat of Substitution *p.125*

RISK
- Macroeconomic
- Competitive Risk

The second pronounced risk in any organization is *competitive risk*. Michael Porter, who also developed the value chaining concepts, developed a tool called the Five Forces to evaluate competitive risk.[20] This tool alone will not make you an expert at competitive threat assessment—but I don't want you to be one. You simply need to become aware, then to understand. This tool will make you aware of competitive risks and help you understand them.

[20]   Michael E. Porter, "How Competitive Forces Shape Strategy," *Harvard Business Review* 59, no. 2 (1979), accessed November 13, 2017, https://hbr.org/1979/03/how-competitive-forces-shape-strategy.

Threat of new entry

On the top of the Y-axis lies the _threat of new entry_ into your market. A new entry is an organization that has essentially the same value proposition as you, with essentially the same business model as you.

Let's say you are part of a New York taxi company in 2005. How much risk of new entries into your market are you exposed to? Very little. You have very little risk, because to gain the right to operate a taxi business in New York City, a person must purchase a medallion that cost (in 2005) over $1 million. The cost of entry into that market was extremely high. Every newcomer to the taxi market had a $1 million up-front expense—before even being able to buy a car!

Therefore, with that business model, there was very low competitive risk from a new entry perspective. On a scale of 1–5, with 1 being _all risk_ and 5 being _no risk_, the threat of new entry for a New York taxi company in 2005 was 4.

Here's another quick example. What do you think is the threat of new entry for a mom-and-pop grocery store in a medium-sized town, when a Big Box company just built a new store in the next town over? I'd say it's a 2, or even a 1. The Big Box store has a wider selection at a dramatically lower cost, which makes it extremely hard to compete with.

Here are some factors influencing the threat of new entry.[21]

* Time and cost of entry

---

[21] These factors and the following ones are drawn from the previously referenced article by Michael Porter.

- Specialist knowledge

- Economies of scale

- Cost advantages

- Technology protection

- Barriers to entry

One group of researchers was curious about what company leaders fear most today. So, they conducted some studies to find out. The researchers asked business leaders, "What aspects of competition do you fear most?" Interestingly, the most common answer did not concern existing competitors. Business leaders were primarily worried about competitors who do not exist today, but will come out of nowhere and hit them in two or three years' time.

In today's world, new entries may successfully compete against long-established firms. Business models are replicated or improved. Business leaders cannot plan many years ahead—that luxury is gone. Staying ahead means adapting quickly, which pressures Green, Blue, and Red alike.

Innovation is difficult for many large organizations, because over the years it has ceased to be part of their DNA. Their culture is used to the status quo. The companies have been built with a command-and-control mindset; they've achieved success by constantly innovating on the small scale.

Think about Intel's historical chip manufacturing process, the "tick-tock model". Each year, Intel strove to complete a "tick" (a shrinking of the process technology) or a "tock" (a new microarchitecture). Those changes consistently improved their microchips.

So far, Intel has innovated well. Yet, think about Nokia, Xerox, and Kodak, companies that failed to embrace change and adapt quickly in the market. Nokia was one of the first companies to develop a smartphone.[22] In 2007, its research and development (R&D) budget was five times larger than Apple's, but bureaucracy and mismanagement of the R&D budget (among other issues) contributed to its downfall.[23] Nokia is no longer the market leader it once was.

Uber is a classic example of disruption. It revolutionized the taxicab market and has permanently changed the transportation industry. Surprisingly, our world is so volatile that the disruptor is now being disrupted in many markets. For instance, in Asia we have Grab, another ridesharing service. Uber disrupted taxi drivers in New York City—now Grab is disrupting Uber in some Asian markets.[24] For example, Jakarta has bad traffic jams. Uber's cars can get caught in traffic. So, Grab introduced GrabBike: You hitch a ride on a motorcycle. The motorcycle can weave in and out, driving around the cars in the traffic jam, helping you to cross the city much faster.[25]

That's one thing I love about Asia: there are many technologies in Asia that have not yet arrived in other parts of the world.

[22]   Sandeep Mehta, "Nokia R&D Spending – A Lesson in Portfolio Balancing," InspiRD, accessed November 13, 2017. http://inspird.com/2011/02/15/nokia-r-spending-lesson-in-portfolio/.

[23]   Kevin J. O'Brien, "Nokia's New Chief Faces Culture of Complacency," The New York Times Company, accessed November 13, 2017. http://www.nytimes.com/2010/09/27/technology/27nokia.html?_r=1&hp.

[24]   Christopher Langner, "Uber, Disrupted," Bloomberg L.P., accessed November 13, 2017. https://www.bloomberg.com/gadfly/articles/2016-04-15/uber-disrupted.

[25]   Muhamad Al Azhari, "Ride Sharing Apps Change the Face of Jakarta's Busy Streets," PT Jakarta Globe Media, accessed November 13, 2017. http://jakartaglobe.id/news/ride-sharing-apps-change-face-jakartas-busy-streets/.

It's just a question of time, though, before innovations there expand to other markets, just as western innovations make their way over there.

It's all about the business model. How can it generate better value for customers? How can it provide a better, more personalized experience? IT technologists are in the middle of it all. They must embrace the willingness to change and lead innovation efforts.

As you strive to be an enabler at your company, realize that innovation is happening all around the world. The world is much smaller than you think it is. Keep your eyes moving around the globe! Learn from innovative foreign companies; apply their strategies to your own business.

Threat of substitution

A new entry is an organization that has essentially the same value proposition as you, with essentially the same business model as you. Now, other organizations have the same value proposition, but reach it in a totally different way—their business model is different. An organization like that is not a new entry, but a *threat of substitution*.

You would think that a nuclear power company would be highly protected from new entries, because of the regulations and technical requirements. And you would be right. If you live in the U.S. and a certain nuclear power company services your state, a new competitor is unlikely to pop up anytime soon. That's not a major threat.

Now, the value proposition of a nuclear power company is *high-quality sustainable electricity at low cost*. Other business models can have that value proposition too. For instance, the number one generator per site of electricity in the world is not nuclear—it's hydroelectric. Nine of the top generators of electricity in the world are hydroelectricity plants.[26] If you can get water to fall and harness its energy, you can generate the most inexpensive electricity. So, in some places hydroelectricity is a substitute for nuclear power. Both deliver the same value, but using diverse technology models.

Substitution is what happened to the taxi companies of New York. Their value proposition is roughly, *we'll get you from point A to point B quickly, cheaply, and easily*. Ride sharing companies said, "We'll do the same thing, but better." Uber and similar ride-sharing companies democratized the taxi industry so that almost anyone could be a driver, then connected those drivers with passengers through apps. That radically changed the taxi companies in New York City forever. Most of them have lost a tremendous amount of equity inside their medallions.

Suppose you were a technologist working for a taxi company when these ride-sharing organizations first began to emerge. If you ran a Five Forces analysis, you could probably identify them as a threat to your company and help develop a rapid response plan. Your company could even invest in Uber to hedge its bets—and that bet would have paid off big time.

To summarize, the two threats on the Y-axis are the *threat of new entry* at top and the *threat of substitution* at bottom. Both

---

[26] Nancy Slater-Thompson and Slade Johnson, "The World's Nine Largest Operating Power Plants Are Hydroelectric Facilities," U.S. Department of Energy, accessed November 13, 2017. https://www.eia.gov/todayinenergy/detail.php?id=28392.

threats are from an organization that shares your value proposition, but a new entry shares your business model while a substitute does not. Risk is measured on a scale of 1–5, with 1 being very exposed and 5 being not at all exposed.

Factors affecting threat of substitution include:

* Substitute performance
* Cost of change

Supplier power

On the left of the X-axis is the *threat of supplier power*. Supplier power corresponds to supplier number—the more suppliers you have, the less power each individual supplier has over you. A sole supplier is administratively easier; plus, you should be able to negotiate a volume discount. The problem is that the supplier eventually comes to have power over you.

Some large chemical companies have a single-source supplier for materials like uranium, which is not exactly plentiful. They simply have to deal with that risk, since diversifying their suppliers is not an option.

Some years back, I founded and managed Firefly, a consulting company that generated revenue through consulting and education activities. The ancient Aztecs considered the firefly to be a source of knowledge in a world of darkness.[27] That's an accurate

---

[27] Diana Marder, "Flash: The True Story Of Lightning Bugs," Chicago Tribune, accessed November 13, 2017. http://articles.chicagotribune.com/1985-08-18/news/8502230870_1_lightning-bugs-flash-abdomen.

description of what we were doing at Firefly: we were educators and illuminators. At Firefly, we had a sole provider of data center space and the automation software that orchestrated our global lab environment. We were closely aligned, and they provided a great service, but having a sole provider for such a critical activity was a substantial risk for us. We had frequent conversations with our supplier to stay on the same page. We even entertained the idea of buying them a few times, to mitigate that risk. Do you have a single-source supplier? Then regularly having open conversations is critical.

A chemical company that has a single-source supplier gets a 1 in risk rating; they have a substantial risk in that product area, as putting all of your eggs in one basket is a high-risk endeavor.

Now consider Walmart, which has a great deal of influence over its suppliers. If Walmart is unhappy and they are not getting the level of service that they need, they can replace suppliers. Since Walmart sells products at a high volume through their stores or online, suppliers are willing to do a great deal to keep that relationship healthy and keep their products selling. The risk of supplier power for Walmart is at 4 or higher, since there is little risk to them.

Factors influencing supplier power include:

- Number of suppliers
- Size of suppliers
- Uniqueness of change
- Ability to substitute
- Cost of changing

Buyer power

On the right side of the X-axis is the *threat of buyer power*. Any organization that represents more than 5% of your revenue has some power over you. If your organization files with the SEC, you must include those organizations when you report risks to your business.

When I first started my consulting company, our first buyer represented 100% of our business. That buyer, whether they knew it or not, had tremendous influence over us. By the time I was ready to sell the company, that same buyer had decreased from 100% to 15% of our thriving business—substantially less risk, though still reportable risk. Any public company in the U.S. has to report when any buyer represents more than 5% of their business revenue.

Think about how much influence your buyers and your suppliers have over you. As a technologist, help your organization mitigate those risks. You can bring practical plans to the strategists and be relevant because you're decreasing the risks they're concerned about.

Factors affecting buyer power include:

- Number of customers
- Size of each order
- Difference between competitors
- Price sensitivity
- Ability to substitute
- Cost of changing

Competitive rivalry

The final threat is the *threat of competitive rivalry.* This is competition from established companies, like Walmart vs. Target or Apple vs. Microsoft or Ford vs. Toyota. Factors affecting this include:

- Number of competitors
- Quality differences
- Other differences
- Switching costs
- Customer loyalty

Completing the analysis

Once you have numbers for the threat of new entries, substitution, buyer power, supplier power, and competition, average them together. That number is the *average risk* for your organization.

To go the extra mile, compare your average to that of your top competitor to see who is more competitive in the marketplace. Assuming your leverage ratios (debt-to-equity ratios) are similar, then whichever company's score is higher should be generating better net income. If your score is higher but you're not generating more income, there's a variable you are not accounting for. Or maybe your business is not leveraging the power you have. Either way, there's an opportunity for you to understand your organization's competitive position better and find innovative solutions.

Risk drives change

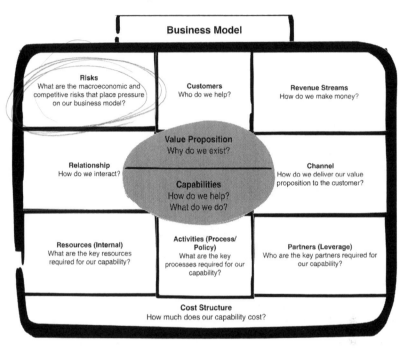

Look at the whole business model. On the top are the value proposition and the revenue it creates. The bottom has capabilities, along with the building blocks for the capabilities and the costs associated with creating them. The combination of value proposition and capabilities is called "packaging," which creates the gross margin. The left includes risks, which oppose the value proposition and lead to change.

That's the key: risk drives change. Organizations alter direction because of external risks. For instance, consider macroeconomic risk—ridesharing companies like Uber, Lyft, Juno, Didi, and Grab pose a threat to traditional transportation services. Some millennials have chosen to rideshare everywhere instead of buying cars and major automobile manufacturers have taken note. This reality demands a change in business model.

Thus, in 2016 General Motors invested $500 million into Lyft. Why? To head off risk by turning Lyft into a partner, including it in the GM business model. Additionally, Lyft has begun renting GM vehicles to Lyft drivers who need a vehicle and take a certain number of trips per week. Lyft is now a part of GM's supply chain, so that even if new car purchases drop off, the ridesharing drivers who replace those purchases will still be driving GM cars. The partnership has come full circle.

For technologists, seeing the connections between GM, Lyft, and the car driver allows us to understand where we can insert technology to enable our business to be successful. Take the almost-certain reality that a future generation of Lyft cars will be autonomous. How can old-school GM technologists partner with born-on-the-Web Lyft technologists to produce and utilize such a vehicle? I don't know the answer, but I know there is one. It's up to the Blue people to find it and when they do, they'll be massively relevant.

customer risk

Linking your projects to risk

Risk to the business model creates the need for change. Green strategists evaluate the needed changes and establish goals. A goal is something that needs to change and it lives at the *top* of the business model: "Increase revenue by 15% this year." That goal requires changes on the *bottom* of the business model. For example:

- Cost structure – Hire salespeople and spend more on salary

- Resources – Replace CRM or update with new module

- Activities – Refine sales process with the help of outside consultant

- Partners – Partner with retail outlets to put our product on their shelves

- Channel – Add an online e-commerce portal to complement direct sales

- Relationships – Create a customer loyalty program for long-term retention and sustainable growth

The one desired change of "Increase revenue by 15% this year" ripples throughout the entire organization. Business initiatives come out of it and lead to the projects we are assigned. We talk about our projects all the time, often not realizing that they came from the rippling impact of a need/change/goal within the business or mission model. *This is why customer buy*

Why does this matter? Because you can link your projects directly to the strategy of your organization, directly to the risks that created this change in the business model. You couch your activities in terms that are relevant to Green's desire for productivity. You become a relevant enabler.

Do you want to have an effective conversation with your Green leadership? Then you must talk about these things. The only business topic that matters is the business model. If you aren't talking about the business model, you should focus on their personal interests (fishing, etc.) because nothing else is relevant. The only thing relevant to your leadership is the business model and the risks and initiatives associated with it. You have to con-

BE RELEVANT

nect your daily work in technology to the business model, like this:

Link all these together and you'll be perceived as relevant to your organization. You'll be able to secure the funding required for your projects. After a great year, you can ask for capital expenditure (CapEx) to beef up the resources required to meet business needs. And if you have a tough year, you'll be able to navigate operational expenditures and keep your organization as healthy as can possibly be.

The key is linking what you do to what they do. That's it. If you link what you do to what Green wants to get done, you are relevant.

p.133

CAPITAL EXPENDITURES (CAPex) → $ spent on FIXED ASSETS [land, buildigs, equipment

OPex ⇒ ongoing costs

Chapter 12.

Financial Analysis

ROI and TCO

comparison

Green strategists spend much time discussing numbers. Technologists don't have to be financial experts but should understand the financial concepts that pertain to their area.

Two frequently used acronyms are ROI and TCO. They stand for Return on Investment and Total Cost of Ownership, respectively. I often hear them used in the same breath, as synonyms, but they are not the same.

The confusion often occurs because technologists are constantly hearing business leaders use these terms without understanding context. The business leader has many investment options which are evaluated with either a hurdle rate or internal rate of return; these are formulas that calculate minimum expected return on any investment. Since no one has ever taught the technologist that a return can only be achieved based on investment with expected cash flows, they may believe that it is just another way of budgeting and that the business leader wants justification for the purchase. Due to the technologist's core focus on efficiency, they interpret the leaders' financial motives as another way to save money. But ROI does *not* mean that.

Total Cost Ownership (TCO) is comparison: we compare one product to another product. This comparison could be between the product we own and something entirely new. We evaluate the variables, like leasing vs. owning. TCO is like comparative shopping. You weigh many variables: location, selection, brand, price, customer service, personal preference.

If someone wants to buy a nice pair of pants at a mall in Dallas, they need to decide where to go. Let's say that they see a Nordstrom's and a Macy's and they are the same distance from each, so location is a tie. Both stores carry the pair of pants they want, so selection is not an issue. Perhaps this person is a lifelong Nordstrom's customer: Nordstrom's will tailor their clothes for free and have extraordinary customer service. This person will pick Nordstrom's unless Macy's can sway them with a 50% discount. That's TCO. According to Forbes, a new competitor's perceived value must be 10x or higher than the incumbent to sway the buyer.[28] *Location, Selection, brand, price, customer service, person*

ROI is not like that at all. Let's say I invest a million dollars into a project with an expected return of $300,000 per year for five years. That will get me $1.5 million in total cash back.

---

[28] Tom Gillis, "Competing With Incumbents: Finding Your 10x," Forbes Media LLC, accessed January 7, 2018. https://www.forbes.com/sites/tomgillis/2011/12/27/competing-with-incumbents-finding-your-10x/#17ac6b9d4940.

Each year I'm making about 10% profit on my money. From a personal investment perspective, that's pretty good. But is that a good move for an organization? An organization has other investment options, like buying technology or train locomotives. The business evaluates potential options based on what the business needs. What are its goals? What results need to be achieved?

The "hurdle rate" is the ROI a project must be expected to meet before it can receive funding. For instance, the business might not invest in any projects below a 10% hurdle rate.

ROI is about cash flow. That's why Green people are much more interested in ROI than they will ever be about TCO (comparison shopping). Those in the Red and Blue worlds, these tactical and operational worlds, care about TCO because they are often short on budget. They need to achieve a result with less money, so they compare. *Green strategies* *Red/Blue - tactical/operational*

ROI and TCO can work together if one understands them correctly. Let's say you want to launch a project with one of your business leaders that will generate 13% ROI and your organization hurdle rate is 10%. If successful, that would greatly benefit your organization, so be sure to *call your shot* as we discussed earlier. Say, "This project will generate 13% ROI." Then do your job well and *hit the mark*. After that, *measure what matters*. If you measure a successfully achieved 13% ROI, that's not only what matters, but extremely relevant. When evaluating suppliers for the project, you will choose from different options, you will use TCO to evaluate different options, and choose the best solution based on the variables (price, availability, etc.) that matter most to the project. *use techniques to design & offer a solution*

Capex vs. Opex

Capex (Capital Expenditure) is an investment. You invest capital dollars into a project which will increase your capabilities and you expect an equal or greater return through that investment. If you are in a commercial organization and your company has had four consecutive quarters of profitability, Capex is essentially free. You are either going to spend it or you are going to pay taxes on it. As you think about the resources needed so that you can support the business model and maintain your capabilities, Capex is a valuable asset. You can use it to shore up your environment and capabilities to be prepared for the next big wave.

Opex (Operational Expenditure) is the necessary expenses to run your organization each day. In a successful organization, you spend operating dollars and earn back more dollars in revenue. Accountants want to match revenue to the expenses used to generate that revenue. Opex is always carefully scrutinized because it generates your operating margins, your EBITDA (earnings before interest, tax, depreciation, and amortization), your net income, and eventually your publicly held EPS (earnings per share). For a private company, the company's worth is typically derived based on a multiplier of EBITDA.

Too many people talk about Capex and Opex without knowing the difference. They don't realize that the net income of the organization is critically important and that the income statement drives many of our business decisions. The income statement holds the organization's revenue and expenses. Capex comes from past profitability that is now available to spend. In fact, if you don't spend your profits then you will be taxed on it. In the US, the corporate tax rate of 2017 was 35%, so at that rate, spending $1 would strengthen the company and effectively cost only $0.65.

You should approach your Green strategist and request Capex during a good year. If your organization has had a poor year, then Capex is just not available. A good year is a good time to shore up internal resources, improve partnerships, and identify opportunities where you should invest heavily. Make capital expenditures at the right time, realizing that money will not be available during a bad year.

Strategic budget thinking

Demystifying ROI, TCO, Capex, and Opex helps us to think strategically. We in IT have historically been handed a budget, told "You have only this much money," and accepted it. Instead, we must realize that budget is derived from the business model. If we aspire to get in the front boat, we need to understand the budget we're being handed. There's no magic about finances. Green strategists are driven by the mission; know that, and you can better decipher the budget they hand you; you can even ask them for what you need.

Lots of Red people in IT believe that efficiency is the main thing, so they work hard all year to save their organization money. The CFO sees those savings and is she impressed? Maybe not. She thinks, "I gave IT too much money! Next year, less." Saving money in IT will not cause the functional leaders to think more of you. That said, if your savings allows your company to make their quarterly numbers, then that reduction in cost will be noticed because your savings has a direct impact on your company's bottom line.

Saving money is good. But simultaneously, if you want to speak Blue and be relevant, you have to get more bang for your buck; effectiveness. Here's an idea for how to use that extra savings to be relevant. Instead of sending the money saved back into the financial coffers, place it into a special budget for you to invest in your functional leaders when they need it. Imagine this: You're sitting in a meeting with a functional leader who says, "I need such-and-such amount of money on top of my own budget so I can purchase this tool and accomplish this goal." You confidently commit: "I'm in. I think that is a great idea and I'm willing to support it from my own budget. I can't float the entire purchase, but I'll be the seed capital."

You've gone from being the person who saves money to the person who invests in the ventures of your functional leaders by supplying seed capital. Your perceived importance will skyrocket. The functional leaders will see you as a relevant Blue enabler. Money talks.

Stop thinking about your budget as something you need to shave money off. Yes, you want to save money, but you want to save so that you can become the venture capitalist of your organization. When your functional leaders are short on funds, you want to be the first person they call. You become the angel investor.

Sometimes, executives give poor incentives to IT, incentives that make saving money seem like the end goal. They say, "If you save money, we'll give you a bonus." That's shortsighted and misguided. Incentives like "Reduce your headcount by 100 and get a 2-million-dollar bonus" are easy to achieve—fire 100 people, regardless of how that affects the organization!

Thankfully, most technologists are not incentivized that way. But they still feel the urge to save money—an urge that must be harnessed. Saving money earns you no relevance *per se*. You can wield your savings as a weapon to win massive relevance by using them as seed capital for functional leaders' projects.

You will never have enough money to provide the full capital, but you can provide the seed capital, and often that's enough. Your interest secures buy-in from other leaders who put their own money on the table. And since you generated that momentum with your seed capital, you receive all the relevance associated with that project.

This brings to mind the concept of the *first follower*,[29] described by Derek Sivers as "what transforms a lone nut into a leader." The first follower is essential to begin a movement and get others on board because he or she gives the leader credibility. Then more adherents join the bandwagon, the more the herd mentality kicks in. IT technologists will not often be the leader, but they can be the first followers to whom the leader will be enduringly grateful.

---

[29] You can view the TED talk by Derek Sivers on the TED website: https://www.ted.com/talks/derek_sivers_how_to_start_a_movement.

Get in the Boat Whiteboard

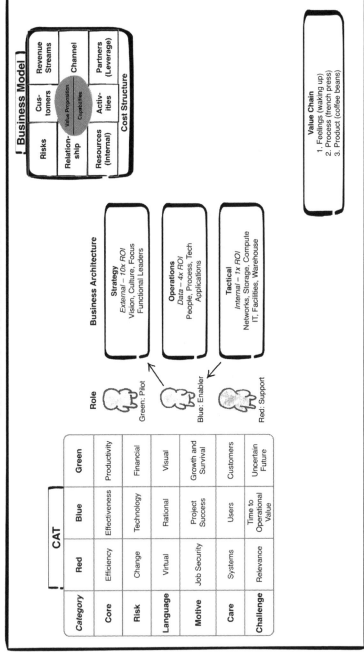

Business Model

Risks	Cus-tomers	Revenue Streams
Relation-ship	Value Proposition	Channel
	Capabilities	
Resources (Internal)	Activ-ities	Partners (Leverage)

Cost Structure

Business Architecture

Strategy
External – 10x ROI
Vision, Culture, Focus
Functional Leaders

Operations
Data – 4x ROI
People, Process, Tech
Applications

Tactical
Internal – 1x ROI
Networks, Storage, Compute
IT, Facilities, Warehouse

Value Chain
1. Feelings (waking up)
2. Process (french press)
3. Product (coffee beans)

Role

Green: Pilot

Blue: Enabler

Red: Support

CAT			
Category	**Red**	**Blue**	**Green**
Core	Efficiency	Effectiveness	Productivity
Risk	Change	Technology	Financial
Language	Virtual	Rational	Visual
Motive	Job Security	Project Success	Growth and Survival
Care	Systems	Users	Customers
Challenge	Relevance	Time to Operational Value	Uncertain Future

SECTION IV.

SPEAK BLUE

Chapter 13.

USIM: Understand and Simplify

Use cases and USIM

ENSURE CLIENTS HAVE THE TECHNOLOGY THEY NEED

→ INNOVATION

The technologist's job is to impact the organization through support and technology. An instance of technology impacting the organization is normally called a *use case*. (Note that saying "Company X used product Y" is not a use case. Some people call it one, but it's actually a *reference*.)

A technology use case is when we use technology to impact the activities of a business. If you look back at the business mod- ← p100 el, an *activity* is a key process required to enable a capability. The use case describes how technology affects that process.

Use cases and processes are inextricably tied together. You cannot present a use case unless you firmly grasp the underlying process. Over the years, I've developed an acronym that helps me with processes: USIM. That stands for Understand, Simplify, Identify, and Measure.

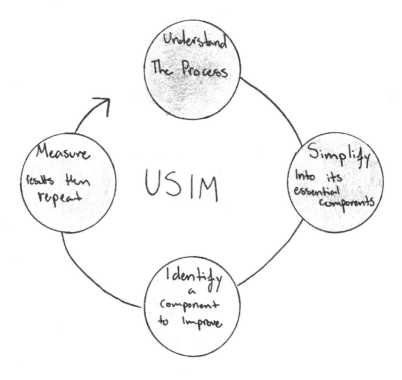

USIM: Understand

First is the need to *understand* the process. In the field of continuous improvement, we use something called the "6Ms" to analyze the parts of a process. These six are:

- Machines

- Methods

- Materials

- Measurements
- Mother Nature
- Manpower

I have simplified those 6Ms for the IT industry, whittling them down to 4 key components:

[handwritten: PERSONNEL] • **Actors**: the people involved directly in the process

[handwritten: APPS] • **Systems**: the applications that drive a process.

[handwritten: ENDPOINTS] • **Machines**: the end points used in the process (i.e., iPad, laptop, mobile phone, ATM machine, etc.)

[handwritten: MANAGEMENT OF THE PROCESS] • **Key Performance Indicators (KPIs)**: the measurements of the process

Using these four components, you can analyze and understand any process. Keeping the four in mind will help you not to forget important aspects of your analysis.

Value streaming: a German coffee tale

Let's talk about coffee again. Earlier, we used coffee to discuss *value chaining*, which is connecting your day-to-day work to the value your organization delivers to end users. Customers who buy coffee want an intangible benefit, such as the aroma or taste of the coffee. Coffee beans are the raw material that produces the intangible benefit. In between the raw material and intangible benefit is a process: maybe a Keurig or a French Press.

Let's stick with this example to introduce the concept of a *value stream*. Value streaming is examining a process to identify where the value is and how it flows throughout the process.

[handwritten: VALUE CHAINING → CONNECTING my WORK TO MY CUSTOMER]
[handwritten: CUSTOMERS]
[handwritten: → CONNECTS TANGIBLE TO INTANGIBLE]

I know the name "value stream" is similar to value chain. To keep them straight, remember that a value chain connects the tangible (raw materials) to intangible (the need or feeling) through a *process*. A value stream is a tool that allows one to see clearly all the critical components of a process and how they fit together. With this tool, the technologist can identify the constraints and opportunities in their process and, most importantly, provide a roadmap to improve that process.

If you go to a coffee shop, one element of their coffee-making process involves various machines: grinders, brewers, and the like. Many people don't realize that coffee companies generally do not take care of their own coffee machines. Maintaining coffee machines is not the core of their business—their core is to make great coffee. They outsource what is not core. The coffee company hires a third party to maintain their coffee machines, just like they outsource AC maintenance.

Let's call the third party that cares for coffee machines a coffee machine managed service provider (MSP). This MSP manages the machines for retail coffee outlets. The average coffee shop has two or three large machines and a handful of smaller ones. Let's call the barista, "Helga." Helga has been working at this shop for a year now and enjoys her job—except when the machines break down.

Helga is an "actor" in the value stream because she has a role to play. When a coffee machine stops working, Helga tries the old trick of turning it off and turning it on again. If that fails to fix the problem, she calls the MSP, whose value proposition is "Call us—we've got your coffee needs covered."

Helga dials the number and is connected to a call center. Hans is an "actor" there, a customer service representative. A call-center application drives the phones and the desktops in the call center. Hans talks with Helga, learns that the coffee machine is down, and then tries to solve the problem over the phone with a simple troubleshooting methodology.

That's the first part of the process. We have two actors: Helga (the customer) and Hans (the customer services representative). Hans works hard but cannot solve the problem remotely, so he needs to dispatch a repair technician.

We in IT sometimes get in trouble because we never work through the exact process. In continuous improvement, this is the idea of "*going to gemba*". Gemba means "the real place" in Japanese. In business, gemba is the place where value is created: a construction site, factory floor, or sales floor. When a business problem arises, going to gemba means going to where the problem is. You can't fix a process from afar. You must understand exactly how it works, up close and personal. Thus, if you are consulting with the MSP, you need to visit the call center and see how it works.

Hans needs to dispatch a technician. How does he do that? It could be physical communication—pick up a phone and call them. But frequently, MSPs with higher volume automate that process. Hans clicks a button inside the call center application that dispatches field services.

That call center button prompts the field services application to create a ticket for field services. Heidi is another "actor," the field services tech. Her job is to receive tickets and go fix machines. She has tools and expertise, but she needs a way to get from here to there. Thus, there's a fleet management application connected to the field services application, so that Heidi can get a vehicle.

Additionally, Heidi will need some replacement parts, which are stored in a warehouse. The warehouse staff pick out those parts for Heidi. To effectively manage that system, there's a warehouse management application that monitors inventory and serves requests to the staff. Heidi gets her vehicle, picks up the needed parts at the warehouse, drives to Helga's store, and repairs the machine.

When it comes to business architecture, many people think there are a few applications and thousands of processes. The reality is that there are only a few processes and many applications; we just analyzed the field services process. A process may contain many standard operating procedures (SOPs), but a procedure is not the same as a process. There are only a few processes in any given business. *Procedures vs Processes*

Value streaming and business model

Let's connect our value stream to the business model. *(Components of the process)* The MSP's *value proposition* is "Call us—we've got your coffee needs covered." The MSP supports that value proposition through the *capability* of repairing broken machines. Capabilities are built from three parts: resources, activities, and partners.

- Hans, Heidi, the truck, and the applications are internal *resources*. *p.109*

- Field service is an *activity*, a key process required for that capability. *p.110*

- The coffee machine manufacturer is a *partner*. *p.110*

KPIs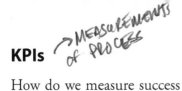

How do we measure success in the field services process? What are the KPIs? Here are a few:

- Call center repairs. How often can Hans fix the problem over the phone?

- Dispatch percentage. How frequently does Hans dispatch a technician to repair a machine?

- Mean time to repair. How long does it take, on average, to repair a machine?

- First-time repairs. Rework is expensive, so we want Heidi to fix the machine correctly the first time.

- Mean time of failure of the coffee machines. How frequently do they break?

- Response time. How much time has elapsed from when Helga calls to when Heidi has finished repairing the machine?

- Technician accuracy. Did Heidi pick up the right parts before heading out on the job?

- Technician utilization. What percentage of time are our technicians being utilized vs unbilled time?

- Vehicle utilization. What percentage of the time are our vehicles in use?

Additionally, customer satisfaction is one of the most critical measurements. It is a *leading* indicator with regard to customer retention, because low customer satisfaction means customers are going to leave and higher customer satisfaction means customers will stay. Customer satisfaction is also a *lagging* indicator with regard to quality, because Helga's satisfaction tells you how good a job Heidi did.

My goal here is to model how you can understand how value flows through a process and how that process connects to the business model. Why does this matter? Because you do not want to *go low* and tinker with the process until you have *gone high* and grasped it as a whole. Do not allow the interesting trees to block your view of the essential forest.

① UNDERSTAND
② USIM: Simplify *INTO ITS MOST / ESSENTIAL COMPONENTS*

Understand is the first step of USIM. The second is *simplify*. Here are a few examples of points in the process that could be simplified.

Data collection: Are we effectively collecting the coffee machine errors inside our own call center application? Is it easy for Hans to mark down what has gone wrong?

Applications: Do we have too many applications? We may need to rationalize a few, collapsing multiple business logic applications into one.

Maintenance: Are we following the preventative maintenance schedule for our vehicles? The technicians should know which vehicles are due for which procedures on a given day.

Distance: How far is Heidi from Helga's store? Large distances increase transportation costs. Third-party distribution centers are a possible solution.

Want to know one of the best ways to simplify a process? "Digital transformation" or "digitization," a current hot topic in the world of IT. The concept of taking something analog and making it digital has been around for a while. Amazon started shipping electronic books for Kindle years ago, for example. These days, everyone is into digitization transformation as a way to leverage technology and stretch each dollar further. Technologists should be at the forefront of enabling our business to make these changes.

[handwritten margin notes: various ways to get more from each dollar]

[handwritten: RED, BLUE & GREEN SEE DIGITAL TRANSFORMATION DIFFERENTLY]

Connecting the unconnected

About a year and a half ago, I bought a Fitbit Blaze. My Fitbit tracks my steps, records my sleeping hours, monitors my heartbeat, and so on. It connected the fundamental components of my health, so I can look at my Fitbit dashboard and get an idea of how I'm doing holistically.

Digitization can connect things you might not expect. Have you heard of CaaS? CaaS is typically short for Containers as a Service, but that's not what I mean. I mean *Cow as a Service*. Yes, you read that right. Think about milk for a minute. The price of milk varies from country to country, but $3.29 was the average U.S. price for 2016.[30] Organic milk costs a few dollars more. For a few people, organic is not enough. They want to know exactly where their milk came from. Capitalists are taking advantage of that desire on some farms in Ireland by putting sensors on cows. In a large production dairy farm, cows are milked by machine. Betsy's sensor is read each time she is milked, and then the milk is

---

[30] "Retail Price of Milk (Fresh, Whole, Fortified) in the United States from 1995 to 2016 (in U.S. Dollars per Gallon)," Statista Inc., accessed November 13, 2017. https://www.statista.com/statistics/236854/retail-price-of-milk-in-the-united-states/.

stamped as hers. Whoever signed up to purchase Betsy's milk receives it soon after, confident that they know exactly where their milk came from. That's connecting the unconnected.

How could we apply this to the coffee MSP? Consider the call center. We could integrate the Customer Relationship Management (CRM) or Enterprise Resource Planning (ERP) systems into the call center application, such that when Helga calls, Hans gets an automatic popup with her store's information. He no longer has to ask for her store's name and location and ID number.

The coffee machines are a prime target for automation. They are unconnected—let's connect them. To do that, we need sensors, which are already embedded in the machines. Next, for those sensors to send outbound communication, we need PLCs—programmable logic controllers. We can install those.

Additionally, we need a network path, a wired or wireless interface inside the copy machines. The machines actually have that too—we just haven't connected them. This is a fabulous opportunity to connect the unconnected. We could connect the coffee machines and begin securely collecting data from their sensors. That real-time data capture enables us to make real-time decisions.

Digitization is not new

ALSO CALLED IoT!

Now, there are many marketing terms around digitization and it's called by many names: "internet of things," "internet of everything". In Germany, it's called Industry 4.0; in Thailand, they call it Thailand 4.0. Despite the complexity, digitization is not new. It actually started with the invention of the transistor in the 1940s. After that, analog started to become digital.

Take sensors, for example. Sensors ten years ago were the size of a shoebox, cost a fortune, measured just a few things, and spoke proprietary protocols. Today's sensors are extremely tiny, can speak wireless, can speak standardized protocols, cost just cents or a few dollars, and can measure many more things. We can put sensors into anything we want. Your mobile phone has many sensors in it. Some companies have even put sensors into forks! Why? So people can measure how fast they eat; the idea is that they might eat more slowly with feedback and thus lose weight.[31] (I have no idea how effective that concept is, but it goes to show you that sensors are everywhere!)

Think about bandwidth. Today, we have 4G everywhere. Well, 10 years ago in most countries, you had no G. No matter where you live, you probably have a decent mobile connection. On a multi-building campus, where 10 megabit or 100 megabit bandwidth was once standard, these network are fast approaching 10 gigabit bandwidth and all available on wireless. In the data center, 100 or 400 gigabit bandwidths are common. Bandwidth has exploded. Compared to a couple of years ago, the world is connected far more extensively and far better.

Computer chips are constantly improving. I don't even know what kind of chip is in my mobile phone. It's an iPhone, so it must be an Apple Ax or something, but I have no clue what version it is or how fast it is. I actually don't care—I don't worry about it because it works. The same is true for my laptop. Computer performance has increased so much that for many applications we don't have to care anymore. It's there if we need it.

Think about storage. Everything used to be hard disk. Now it's flash storage and it's much faster. Solid-state drives (SSDs) are

---

[31] You can check out this product at https://www.hapi.com/product/hapifork.

everywhere. Form factors have shrunk. The volume we can store has increased exponentially.

If you look at databases and big data (e.g. Hadoop, SAP HANA, new SQL versions from Microsoft), everything today can be cached in large volumes at real-time speed. 10 years ago, we would have struggled to access this type of data and certainly instant access was impossible. But today, real-time visibility is no longer the future, but fast becoming table stakes.

Think about artificial intelligence (AI) and machine learning. Technologists have been playing around with AI for 30–40 years. But now they are causing tremendous progress. For instance, a computer has now beaten a master at Go, a complex board game that originated in ancient China.[32] Beating a master at chess simply requires a lot of number crunching and following a set of simple rules. But in Go the state space is large enough that just number crunching isn't feasible. Intelligent software is essential.

Digitalization means that because of these underlying technologies, we have the capability to connect the unconnected: sensors, users, databases, artificial intelligence, applications. Connecting the unconnected drives new business models and personalizes customer experiences. That's ultimately what digitalization means: connecting the unconnected to generate new value for customers.

DIGITIZATION ALLOW THE CONNECTED TO BE CONNECTED TO GENERATE NEW VALUE FOR CUSTOMERS

---

[32] Reuters, "Computer Beats Chinese Master in Ancient Board Game of Go," Telegraph Media Group Limited, accessed November 13, 2017. http://www.telegraph.co.uk/news/2017/05/24/computer-beats-chinese-master-ancient-board-game-go/.

Chapter 14.

USIM: Identify and Measure

The final steps of USIM are Identify and Measure.

USIM: Identify

The third step is *identify*. Have you simplified the process into its essential components, removing extraneous steps? Excellent. Now you should identify a component to improve.

Identification is about continuous improvement. Do not try to change every aspect of the process at once, lest you never know what caused the improvement (or disaster). Follow these three steps:

- ☑ Establish a baseline
- ☑ Change something
- ☑ Measure the result

Then repeat! Keep on identifying things to improve. Adhering to this process lets you increase the speed of how many changes you make, while still understanding the impact of each individual change.

USIM: Measure

Before you improve a process, set a baseline for your current state, then, iterate. Modify one thing at a time and measure the difference. If you change more than one thing at a time, you will never know which one caused the positive (or negative) effect.

Once we automate the coffee machine connection, that should change a lot of things. Mean time to repair should decrease, since we know the instant a machine is down. Helga doesn't even have to pick up the phone. And the machine gives us data on what is broken, so our repair accuracy should increase. We can also perform better preventative maintenance, because the machines can notify us when they are due for cleaning or a replacement part. Best of all, we can carry out *predictive* maintenance, monitoring the status of each machine and proactively fixing issues before they break the machine.

More fundamentally, the value proposition of the business will change. "Call us—we've got your coffee needs covered" is now outdated, in a very positive way. The customer doesn't even have to call anymore! The machine does the calling and Heidi shows up ready to fix it in no time flat.

To speak Blue, we need to understand the processes we work in daily. I use the MSP example because many organizations have field services and their value streams would look similar. Now, the machines might change. The actors might change. The applications or systems might change but the underlying process would look similar.

So, that's one example of a value stream. The acronym USIM helps us follow the value throughout the process. You need to _understand_ the key components: understand the actors, understand the systems, understand the machines, and understand the KPIs. _Simplify_ the systems to reduce unnecessary complexity. _Identify_ a component to improve. Then, _measure_ your success.

To use USIM and improve a process, do you need to be the expert at process engineering? No. You really just need to be curious. Your fellow Blue people that work in sales, production, etc know their area very well, they just need your help to figure out how to use technology in an even more impactful way. The goal should be to improve your listening, to be an enabler, and to facilitate a deeper understanding of your company's business processes. Work together to connect the unconnected and provide better visibility for your organization.

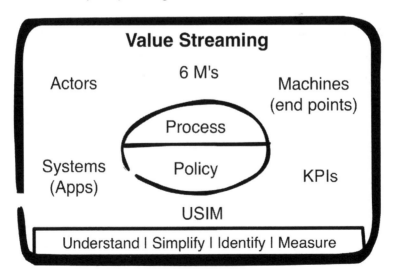

Get in the Boat Whiteboard

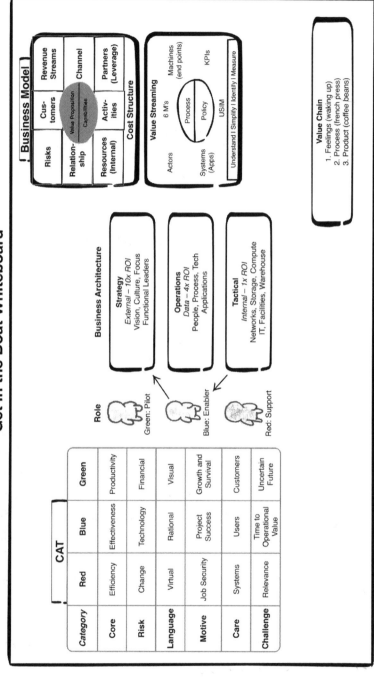

Business Model

Risks	Cus-tomers	Revenue Streams
Relation-ship	Value Proposition Capabilities	Channel
Resources (Internal)	Activ-ities	Partners (Leverage)

Cost Structure

Value Streaming

6 M's — Machines (end points)

Actors — Process — KPIs

Systems (Apps) — Policy

USIM

Understand I Simplify I Identify I Measure

Value Chain
1. Feelings (waking up)
2. Process (french press)
3. Product (coffee beans)

Business Architecture

Strategy
External – 10x ROI
Vision, Culture, Focus
Functional Leaders

Operations
Data – 4x ROI
People, Process, Tech
Applications

Tactical
Internal – 1x ROI
Networks, Storage, Compute
IT, Facilities, Warehouse

Role

Green: Pilot

Blue: Enabler

Red: Support

Category	Red	Blue	Green
Core	Efficiency	Effectiveness	Productivity
Risk	Change	Technology	Financial
Language	Virtual	Rational	Visual
Motive	Job Security	Project Success	Growth and Survival
Care	Systems	Users	Customers
Challenge	Relevance	Time to Operational Value	Uncertain Future

CAT

Chapter 15.

Competitive Advantage

The Advantage

How does the technologist use their ability to positively impact their company's business processes and have a direct impact on their business model? It's not as hard as it might seem. According to Chan Kim and Renée Mauborgne in their well-known book <u>Blue Ocean Strategy</u>, there is a clear path to do this. Not to be confused with the Blue and Red People in this book, Kim and Mauborgne also used colors to indicate the state of the particular market when he referred to "red oceans" and "blue oceans". A red <u>ocean</u> is an ocean full of sharks; full of blood. It is incredibly competitive and difficult to navigate and to survive in. A blue <u>ocean</u> is clear sailing; no sharks, no competitive

RED OCEAN — SHARKS
BLUE OCEAN — NO SHARKS, NO COMPETITIVES

pressures. Another way to look at this personally is like this: let's assume that you are very good at a specific task, for instance, being a highly skilled troubleshooter, but you are poor at marketing. What should you do? Improve your skill at marketing? Most people focus on what they are poor at and try to improve it. Taking the time to do this will reduce the time that can be spent improving strengths. The result of this is mediocrity. Your marketing may improve but you haven't spent time honing the skills that could set you apart...and you enter shark infested waters.

What's a better way? First off, we need to figure out if our strengths have any correlation with our weaknesses. In this particular case, it would. Your strong troubleshooting skills are needed as a technologist but if no one knows you have the skills, that's a problem. Rather than abandoning your craft to pursue marketing, you should work with someone else who already possesses the needed marketing skills so that you can focus your time on improving your specialty. The market demand for your skills would skyrocket due to your laser focus.

Focus on strengths

Delegate weakness or jobs considered support

A company's value is communicated through their value proposition. Lego's value proposition is that they teach children problem solving skills. If Legos improved their value proposition, they would be even more laser focused in their particular market and more successful. In our coffee machine MSP example, their value proposition was, "Call us, we have your coffee needs covered." By eliminating the "Call us," aspect, our MSP's value proposition radically improved. However, this is not enough. You must simultaneously eliminate cost to radically improve the MSPs market position.

According to Kim and Mauborgne, you must do the following:

What is our value proposition? Provide end-to-end IT Solutions & Professional Services to drive digital transformation

→ WHAT IS TOP OF MIND FOR CUSTOMERS

- Raise – Which factors should be raised well above the industry's standard? *↳ SECURITY & WIRELESS,*

- Reduce – Which factors should be reduced well below the industry's standard?

And:

- Create – Which factors should be created that the industry has never offered? *✱ FA REG. PROCESS*

- Eliminate – Which factors that the industry has long competed on should be eliminated?

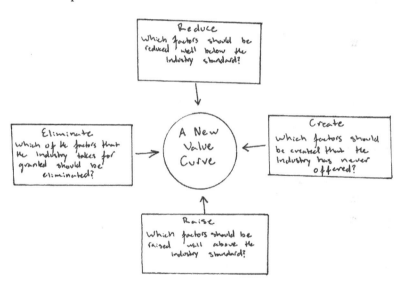

A great example that Kim and Mauborgne use is Cirque du Soleil. Cirque du Soleil is a circus, but not a traditional one. Back in the 1980s, Guy Laliberté and Gilles Ste-Croix (the co-founders) thought to themselves, "We like the circus. We like acrobats and dancing and music. Let's ramp those up radically. And let's eliminate all the other costs: no animals, no star performers." They also got rid of the English language—in fact, every language. This unexpected move gave them access to a worldwide labor pool, dramatically reducing costs.

Kim and Mauborgne say, "Cirque du Soleil succeeded because it realized that to win in the future, companies must stop competing with each other. The only way to beat the competition is to stop trying to beat the competition."

With Cirque du Soleil, Laliberté and Ste-Croix set sail in an ocean free of sharks and have been incredibly successful for over 30 years. Why? Because they carved out a model that is uncon-tested. *IDENTIFY MARKETS* And what happened to the competition? On May 21, 2017, the Ringling Bros. and Barnum & Bailey Circus closed after 146 years. The traditional circus model was no longer sustainable.

What if you could help your organization shift into uncontested waters? Say you work for the coffee machine MSP. You propose, "We should enable ourselves to carry out predictive maintenance instead of repairing broken machines. We can do this by connecting the unconnected machines through sensors and networks. This will dramatically reduce costs while improving our value proposition and increasing our appeal to customers." You call your shot and then hit the mark. How relevant would you be? More than you've ever been.

Remember the paradox from earlier? Technology is more relevant than it has ever been, yet technologists are still not in the boat with the business leaders. You can grow in relevance by positively impacting your organization through value streaming with blue ocean strategy. You can understand a business process, identify areas to improve, amplify your organization's value, and shift it toward uncontested waters. That's being Blue.

PREDICTIVE PROACTIVE SOLUTIONS BY CONNECTING THE UNCONNECTED MACHINES

Power of Blue

Alexander Braumann, a friend of Robert's from Austria, discusses his experience in the Blue World:

> *I joined Cisco in December 2000 via a trainee program and it didn't take long until I went into the field of IP Telephony—now called the "Collaboration unit". Let me tell you a story about one of my first experiences on the power of Blue, of translating "technology into business".*
>
> *It all started when I met the CIO of an Austrian customer about six years ago. From the beginning, we connected and I really enjoyed working with him. At that time, I was a Collaboration Systems/Sales Engineer at Cisco Austria. This CIO really understood the key to success in any end client project was user experience and since all communication impacted every user process, whether it was by video or by voice, it was critical that we got it right. The other thing that this CIO truly understood was that technology is essentially a dead weight without the user adopting it in their daily life.*
>
> *The CIO had some very specific ways that he directly enabled his business. First off he made it clear that we could not use nerd/tech language. Second, he asked us to always understand the business problem we were solving – what business processes were we directly impacting with our collaboration solution. He would tell us, "My company is a speedboat and it is my job to equip this agile boat for future waves." He got it! He understood that not only was technology required to solve an actual business problem, but if he was ever to be allowed in the boat – he would need to have direct impact.*

USER EXPERIENCE

Many people in the IT industry find it easy to understand and communicate the value of collaboration tools while also finding it difficult to communicate the value of other IT solutions, such as networking and performance monitoring tools. There is a simple explanation. Collaboration involves people and quite often involves user applications and processes. Collaboration is blue. That is good news! The technologist is already involved in areas that directly impact the Blue and Green world.

Robert Schaffner bridges the gap between worlds in Singapore:

> *You can use collaboration to pivot from Red to Blue within a project. I remember a story about Singapore American School, a customer of my systems integrator company. Our project with the school was rather technical: replacing the private branch exchange (PBX) with an alternative solution. Thankfully we completed the project successfully and speedily.*
>
> *As soon as the new technology was in place, we engaged with people at the school about how to fully take advantage of it. What could we do with this technology? How could we improve the students' experience? Could we enable sick students to connect into the classroom? Suddenly, we were in Blue conversations with the school and that collaboration led to several fruitful projects.*

[handwritten margin note: KNOWLEDGE TRANSFER / TRAINING]

Role Confusion

Blue operators must be able to communicate and partner with Green strategists, lest the organization fall apart. My friend Justin

Brady told me he had firsthand experience with this. Here is his story of what can happen when Blue is not in the boat.

I started out my career as an engineer working with networks and voice solutions. A man named Ben was my mentor and though he was not the CEO, for all intents and purposes he ran the company.

A few years later, I started to run down the Blue path. I asked Ben how I could do things differently, how I could help out clients, and how I could do some business consulting. That eventually led to a few different positions: running our network operations center, our project engineering group, and our cloud services division.

In turn, those positions migrated into some responsibility in the Green area. Along with Ben, I was responsible for projections for the entire company: looking at company financials, and helping set the company vision.

The interesting part of this story concerns the company's CEO and part owner, whom we will call Albert. During his last few years at our company, Albert began to step out of the day-to-day operations. Although he was the CEO, he wasn't providing vision and he wasn't providing direction, at least from my standpoint. He was basically leaving all the responsibility to Ben. Ben was informing Albert the CEO about vision and structure and strategy.

Albert had also continued to be loose with company expenses. We began to notice many questionable expenses. These weren't small numbers, either. Some expenses were purchased in his name only but paid for with company money. Oftentimes he would have egregious expenses and write it off to different clients. He might have a quick meeting with a client and then spend large amounts of company money on unrelated expenses and state they occurred because of the meeting and that the client participated in them when that was not always the case.

Albert decided to launch a new division in the company and long story short, it failed after a couple of years, but not before costing the company a large amount of money. It's my opinion that this had put the company into a cash poor state. We then began to see real signs of company trouble. The business started sliding. Clients started to notice negative changes as well. This is where the disconnect between Green and Blue really started to have a negative impact. Ben, along with myself, took the initiative to try and arrest the slide. Our company's existing board agreed to step down, and we brought a new board into the company. This board consisted of three individuals who specialized in taking companies of our size and growing them an average of 3x-4x and beyond. Between them, they had successfully done this many times.

A few months into the new board's tenure, Albert was removed as the CEO and Ben replaced him as the CEO. At this point, I would describe it as a battle between Green and Blue. It seemed like Green was trying to drown Blue with their boat. During this time Ben spent most of his time dealing with internal issues related to this and was really challenged to perform his job in resetting the vision of the company. The new Board worked with Ben to develop a plan to turn the company around and set it up for future success and growth.

In another few months, the board presented their plan right before Thanksgiving. This is where things took a turn for the worse. Albert has a knack for convincing one that his way is right and everyone else's is wrong. He is really good at this. He *throws promises out left and right and in my case almost never came through. He really knows how to get you behind him and support him.*

The ownership (previous board) reviewed the plan as the changes proposed required majority vote and they decided they did not want to pursue that plan and dictated several things that had to be done. One of these included laying off about 40% of the staff in order to make the company immediately profitable. The board had stated that would be detrimental to the business and said they could not support any plan other than the one they had presented after almost a year of deliberation.

Nevertheless, the owners rejected the board's plan. The board had no recourse other than to resign. The owners took over again as board members, which put the company into a state of flux for about a week. None of us outside of those owners knew what would happen next.

The week after Thanksgiving, Ben got a call from one of the owners. The board was relieving Ben of his duties and letting him go, effective immediately.

Two days later, the board members brought in a new outside individual as CEO. I can only assume they had been searching for a new CEO over the past few weeks or months to act that fast. It's my opinion that the board already knew what they were going to do before that Thanksgiving meeting.

Shortly after, the new CEO identified individuals to lay off, encompassing about 40% of the company. I made it clear that if we laid off these individuals, the employees who were left would have to work 80-hour weeks and would risk more employees leaving due to the uncertainty. I also stated that I didn't think we could sustain the level of service needed to our clients to continue to grow. Nevertheless, the decision was out of my hands. I personally had to lay off 11 employees (the vast majority of those laid off) that day. He did take other's feedback into consideration during this, but as I later found out, the new CEO just didn't have the information he needed coming into the business and later resigned 3-4 months later. One of the owners took over as CEO.

A few weeks after that, I quickly realized that the damage had been done. A lot of relationships had been suffering during the last year of company chaos. Communication was basically non-existent. The result of this was that many employees were unsure of everything. As a result, client relationships also suffered and the mentality became just holding on to a job as opposed to delivering the value and culture of the company we had in years past. Clients noticed this and as a result, some clients ended their relationship with the company.

In the end, just 6 months later, the board members called an all-hands meeting. They stated that as of the end of the day, the company was closing its doors. That same day, the owner turned CEO started calling clients with the message that as of the end of the day, the company was closing its doors and it would no longer be able to provide the level of support in which they were accustomed. That threw my world into chaos as I received calls from many clients and employees seeking advice and help.

Sometime later, with my new company, I attended a training hosted by Pat Bodin. As he talked about Green, Blue, and Red people, I could correlate all the different parts of my story to relational breakdown between the different colors. Specifically, there was a complete breakdown between Green and

Blue. The Blue board presented a plan to save the company, but the Green owners told them to cut 40% of the staff. The Blue board tried to explain that drastic cuts would most likely kill the company, but the Green owners insisted on that route. The line between Green and Blue were completely blurred. Those who thought they were green, were actually blue (by definition). They were just providing recommendations while the true Green (the owners) had to approve the direction. Throughout this story, role confusion was in full swing. All the major warning signs in the next section were present throughout. The key lesson here is that ownership always wins out in the end—even to the detriment of a company, unfortunately.

Warning Signs

Here are a few warning signs of company downfall. Do you perceive any of these in your business? If so, it needs to enhance the relationships between Green and Blue and Red, in line with the principles taught in this book.

Disconnected Green leaders is a warning sign of a company's downfall. The C-Suite needs to stay involved and understand how the business operates. When Green dictates what will happen, without input from Blue and Red, disaster is just over the horizon.

Poor communication or lack of communication is another warning sign. As the company was falling apart, the owners thought they were keeping the problems hidden from everyone outside the immediate fray. They thought the engineers and technologists were in the dark. But they didn't realize that people talk in organizations. People notice change, especially change for the worse.

> *In the heyday of my company, we had lines of communication open. People listened. But during the last few years of the company's life, people stopped listening. Employees would bring issues and ideas to Ben and me, but we could never get buy-in from the owners and board. Company meetings turned from dialogues into monologues: "This is what you're going to do. Here's what you have to do it with. Now go do it." There was no two-way communication, only dictation about how things were going to happen.*

Employee unhappiness is the final warning sign. In an environment where Red and Blue people feel irrelevant, employees stop saying, "I am here to work for the good of the business," and start saying "I am here to do the minimum work and go home."

That is a disaster recipe for any business. You don't ever want your employees to have that mindset. You want them to have pride in their work. At my business, we always prided ourselves on how we helped our clients. We tried to train our Red people to speak Blue. We told them, "Whenever you're with a customer, always ask how you can improve the relationship between them and us—even if it's not part of your job description. Always be thinking that way. And if you have any ideas yourself, let us know."

Communication breakdown between Green and Blue and Red spells disaster. That's why it is so crucial that you learn how to be relevant and get in the boat.

Summary

The key to successfully being Blue is relevance to the goals of the organization. The strategists and the tacticians don't typically communicate well. The role of Blue people is to enable the strategists' business model and use the support of the tacticians to accomplish their mission. If Blue people connect the dots effectively across the organization, there will be less friction and more success. They do that in two ways. First, they understand the value chain: the coffee beans go through the French press and create the benefits of aroma, flavor, and social interaction. The Blue person ensures there are no missing links between what the business needs and the tactical solutions to those problems by making sure the processes and policies of the organization work together in unison.

Blue people delve into specific processes to improve them. This is called value streaming. (In the coffee example, value streaming is trying to improve the French Press.) They look at the process as a whole, see how diverse elements fit together, and implement practical, tactical changes in order to better the outcome. This affects the value of the entire process, helps achieve specific KPIs, and promotes organizational goals. Blue people call their shot beforehand, hit the mark with their changes, and measure what matters on the back end. As they enable the organization to meet its goals, Blue people are increasingly seen as relevant by Green strategists.

To effectively improve a process, Blue operators need to understand the desires of the Green strategists. That is why understanding the business model and what drives it is important. Green strategists ponder those matters regularly. Technologists can directly engage in a process within an organization and if they can make the process more effective, they can also make the experience more impactful.

Here's the challenge: historically, technologists have spent little time thinking about business models and value streaming. They have only cared about and worked with the raw ingredients. The idea that the technologist should be thinking about business models and value streaming is probably new to you, but I think it is essential. I would like technologists everywhere to spend a lot of their "mind time" thinking about value streaming. Value streaming empowers you to plug into a process and improve it, which is the number one way you can become relevant. No better way exists. What if the technologist was no longer viewed as the roadblock, but started to *be viewed as the competitive advantage of their company?*

position my role as the companies differentiator

SECTION V.

ELEVATE RED

Chapter 16.

Are You a Lone Wolf?

A habit is a labor-saving device for your brain—and once it finds one, it doesn't like to let it go. In his book The Power of Habit, Charles Duhigg says that habits emerge "Because the brain is constantly looking for ways to save effort. Left to its own devices, the brain will try to make almost any routine into a habit, because habits allow our minds to ramp down more often."[33]

Once a habit is established, it is very difficult to break. Anyone who has ever tried to change their dietary norms or start an exercise routine knows this. We might call the phenomenon "habit inertia". We continue along with the same habits because it is easier, it is a well-worn path.

Habits are not only physical activities like brushing your teeth or going to the gym. Habits are also mental activities like "Don't trust strangers," or "Think concretely instead of abstractly." There

---

[33] Patrick Lencioni, *The Five Dysfunctions of a Team: A Leadership Fable* (San Francisco: Jossey-Bass, 2002).

is a common mental habit in IT that must be eliminated before a Red person can be elevated to Blue. We might call it the *lone wolf perspective*.

SALES TEAM

Wolves are pack creatures. They prefer to live and hunt together, which enables them to take down animals larger than themselves. But sometimes a wolf leaves the pack and heads out on its own; it becomes a "lone wolf". Since they must fend for themselves, these animals are often more aggressive and dangerous.

Technologists often view themselves as lone wolves outside the pack. That perspective is both self-made and group-facilitated through habit and inertia. The mindset is "us against the world," which makes working effectively with others quite difficult. Lone wolves don't put themselves in vulnerable positions. Why? Because they have no support from a pack. And since they are not willing to show vulnerability, no other pack will ever invite them to join with them.

Patrick Lencioni, whom we met earlier as the author of The Three Signs of a Miserable Job, wrote a business fable called The Five Dysfunctions of a Team. Here is his list of dysfunctions:

❶ Absence of trust—lack of willingness to be vulnerable within a group

❷ Fear of conflict—preferring artificial harmony over constructive passionate debate

❸ Lack of commitment—feigning buy-in for group decisions, which promotes ambiguity in the group

❹ Avoidance of accountability—letting peers slide into counterproductive behavior without challenging them, which sets low standards

⑤ Inattention to results—focusing on personal success (such as status and ego) before team success[34]

The fundamental dysfunction is the absence of trust; nothing happens without trust. Lencioni writes, "Great teams do not hold back with one another. They are unafraid to air their dirty laundry. They admit their mistakes, their weaknesses, and their concerns without fear of reprisal."[35] Elsewhere, he notes that "Teamwork begins by building trust. And the only way to do that is to overcome our need for invulnerability."[36]

Forming bonds

There is a reason that teamwork is good for us. There is a reason that knowing each other, working hard together, and being successful together is more impactful than seeking success individually. And it's not just about being relevant, which provides meaning in our work; there is something more. Carl Jung stated, "Until you make the unconscious conscious, it will direct your life and you will call it fate." The hidden secret is that our behavior is directed in part by unconscious forces.

As discussed earlier, Patrick Lencioni states that one of the signs of a miserable job is anonymity; we must know the people we work with on a personal level or we'll be unhappy. This is one of our challenges with other co-workers in our organization; we may not know them. Scientists have noted the "proximity

---

34 Ibid.

35 Ibid.

36 Ibid.

principle," the tendency for people who work closely together or live near each other to develop friendly relationships over time. It is thought that this is due to our brain's need to group things together, to mentally assign objects (including people) which are in close proximity to each other into a shared group. Repeated interaction with people in near proximity actually creates connection in our minds, especially if there are also shared goals, values, or experiences. Our brain groups ourselves together when given the opportunity, causing individuals, "I and me," to become a unit, "we and us". Working individually detracts from this. Spending too much time working from home has the potential to detract from this.[37]

When we do form positive relationships and start to effectively work together, our body will make an even stronger bond with a neurotransmitter called oxytocin. Oxytocin is the warm and fuzzy chemical, the "love hormone" responsible for creating attachments and establishing trust. But here is the thing about oxytocin – it doesn't just give us a feeling of well-being, it is produced by our brain's response to anything that feels good to us, whether physical or mental. Are you eating a delicious dessert? Your body produces oxytocin. Were you just embraced by a loved one? Oxytocin. Greeted by your puppy at the end of the day? Oxytocin. Given credit by a coworker? Oxytocin. Praised and recognized by someone in leadership, especially in a public setting? Oxytocin. Our workplaces are becoming increasingly virtual with less time to have in-person proximity, fewer opportunities to talk around the water cooler, and less opportunity to "break bread" with our co-workers. The virtual workplace can have benefits to families and individuals, which can increase job satisfaction, but care must

---

[37] Newcomb, T.M. (1960). Varieties of interpersonal attraction. In D. Cartwright & A. Zander (Eds.), "Group dynamics: Research and theory"

be taken to avoid the potential negative side-effects of separation. How do we mitigate this fragmentation? The more we can do to increase both our virtual proximity and our actual proximity, the better our team will function; texting is less proximal than voice calling and voice calling is less proximal than video chatting, for instance. The more we can share the credit with our group, the more public praise we can give, the healthier we will be as individuals and as a team, because our brain chemistry matters.

Serotonin and dopamine are two other chemicals that contribute to job satisfaction. Serotonin is a neurotransmitter responsible for mood. When people feel low social support, they have lower serotonin levels and will feel less job satisfaction. It is important to feel part of a group, to work as a team. Dopamine is responsible for motivation and the high we get from meeting goals. One of the things that I love about being a technologist is the thrill of solving a problem that was viewed by many as unsolvable or at least difficult. When we reach success on these projects, our body kicks in dopamine.

So, with the proximity principle in place, enhanced by our brain chemistry, how do we use that to get in the boat with leadership? We need to seek ways to get out of our comfort zone and engage systematically with people that have a common goal, our company's success, but not a common role. Technologists need to talk to others in the organizations, such as sales, marketing, engineering, production. Technologists are often introverts and this takes bravery on their part, but remember that Blue people don't bite. Taking baby steps toward this goal is fine as long as steps are being made.

Technologists cannot survive as lone wolves. The IT department's only hope is a shift in perspective from outsider to insider and from lone wolf to valued partner. As one sage proverb ex-

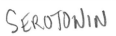

presses it, "If you want to go fast, go alone. If you want to go far, go together."

Chapter 17.

What Do You Fear?

[handwritten: → THE UNKNOWN]

What do technology leaders fear? I believe the most common fear is *the unknown*. Specifically, it's the unknown future state that any change might bring about: "What if the business changes and my job is no longer valuable? What if my amazing boss leaves and a bad one replaces him then makes my life miserable?" What if…what if…what if. As a consequence, adrenaline, the flight-or-fight response, engages. Most technologists prefer flight: You hide from the higher-ups and hope you can do a satisfactory job without getting fired. *[handwritten: ✳ SO TRUE]*

What happens when you hide from fear? It directs your life without you realizing it. Carl Jung was a Swiss psychiatrist who founded a school of psychology around the 1920s. He addressed being conscious to fear: "Until you make the unconscious conscious, it will direct your life and you will call it fate."[38] Hiding

---

[38]   C.G. Jung, "Quotes," Goodreads Inc., accessed November 13, 2017. https://www.goodreads.com/author/quotes/38285.C_G_Jung.

from fear places you in the realm of fate. You are no longer in control. You do not mitigate *risk* because that risk, to your unconscious mind, seems like uncontrollable *fate*. You are subjugated to the outcome.

What is the smart way to handle fear? You identify the risk and mitigate it. Carl Jung would describe that process as *becoming conscious*. I think "conscious fear" is just another name for "risk," and the good news is that you can mitigate risk. Open your eyes to new opportunities.

For instance, your boss might leave the company, which causes you fear because he provides protection and relationship. Once you identify the fear as a *risk of lost relationship*, you can respond by expanding your network to include others in the organization. You endeavor to become relevant, asking, "How can I impact you in a positive way?" Extending your umbrella of protection, you gain new relationships and mitigate the risk of your boss leaving. With a new network of relationships, you are more relevant, have a better career path, and have more leverage to ask for a budget.

> EXPAND RELATIONSHIPS OUTSIDE OF NORCROSS.

Our natural reaction

Our natural reaction to the uncertain future threatens to derail our efforts to get into the same boat. How? Because our natural reaction is fear and while we are afraid, we are bad teammates.

How do people respond when confronted with an uncertain future? The psychological framework is *flight or fight.* I've seen this throughout my career. IT people hide from their own business. Even for leaders, this is not uncommon! This, of course, creates communication challenges, because leaders who are controlled by fear don't want to talk to anyone. They are already afraid of failing at their current projects, so why would they want to talk to someone who might give them another one? Visualize a desk covered by stacks of paper in piles that reach above the head. The technology leader is thinking, "Everything will topple over if I add another piece of paper." Whether that is the reality or not does not make a difference if that is the perception of the mind.

I've been in many environments where the Director of IT has a list of all his projects on the whiteboard behind him and the entire board is covered with scrawled listings of projects. He doesn't even know how he's going to prioritize this workload, much less complete all of these projects. How do technology leaders operate in such an environment? By squeaky wheels and pet projects. "The squeaky wheel gets the grease," and the loudest-shouting functional leader gets the IT help. As for pet projects, they may prioritize (consciously or unconsciously) what they really want to work on instead of what is most necessary for the business. Thus, a disconnect emerges.

Is competency the issue? I don't think so. There are some incompetent people out there, but I think the issue is prioritization, not competency. The challenge is to prioritize our work to make sure we're doing the right things and not hiding from the functional leaders who could tell us what those "right things" are. Even if they communicate clearly, our own fear can shut down our listening abilities so that we don't hear well.

Sometimes technology leaders do opt for fight over flight. This frequently happens to avoid having to say those dreaded, three words: "I don't know." Technology leaders want to stay away from that phrase, never admitting ignorance. Technologists commonly believe their value is derived from what they know.

Because of this, they hold their knowledge hostage and resist the free exchange of ideas with others.

Moreover, they hate to be contradicted. When someone dares to contradict them, they emerge from hiding and try to prove that they know better. And maybe they did know better than everyone else 30 years ago. Today, almost every young leader has a decent idea of technology's capabilities. The leader knows the desired outcome and that it can be achieved but just doesn't know how exactly to achieve it. So, when IT says "It can't be done," the response is skepticism. The leader knows someone can do it, often because he has experienced it in the business-to-consumer (B2C) world. Technological progress brings new features along all the time. Young leaders know that they can integrate family members' schedules together into a shared calendar, they are aware of the encrypted messaging that now comes standard on many smartphones; they have witnessed these functionalities and many others in B2C, so they question why their technologists can't replicate that functionality within the business. They say, "I need encrypted messaging" and hear back, "It can't be done." They are in disbelief. "What do you mean it can't be done? My smartphone does it. Why can't you?"

Now the IT person feels threatened and justifiably so. They thought their knowledge would give them job security but watch as leaders look at outside the company to solve their problems, putting their livelihood at risk. The technologists' protected knowledge is being questioned, so they come out ready for a fight to prove they know better. The business leader is confused by this response. All he is trying to do is attain a result but, instead, what he got back is a fight. Now the relationship is full of tension.

Here is the fundamental misconception to which many technologists fall prey. Historically, value has been based on knowledge. That is not the case anymore. Wikipedia and YouTube alone have made loads of knowledge accessible to all. Today, value is not based on what you know but rather it is based on what you can do with what you know. We might say that the new requirement is knowledge plus experience, which equals wisdom.

Technologists need to admit when they don't know something, then go look for the answer. And when they do know, refusing to share is not the way to go. Sequestering knowledge, even from a desire for job security, is a losing strategy. As technologists erect a hedge of protection around their proprietary knowledge, so will others. Over time their knowledge will become less valuable and more ancient and no one will share their updated information with each other.

Are you conscious to your fear?

→ WHAT IS MY FEAR?

We are mostly unconscious to our fear. Thus, we make no changes to address it. Our decisions are made in a vacuum and only perpetuate the current state. We're driftwood in a river; we'll continue to float where the river takes us until we assert control and exert force to move in a positive direction. Unconscious fear is fate—conscious fear is *risk*.

Conscious fear is not pleasant but can be counteracted by repeatedly taking steps to face and overcome it. My wife and I live in a city with a snaking river and multiple bridges. When we first moved here, she had a phobia of driving over bridges and it is nearly impossible to get anywhere in town without driving over a bridge or two. Although she has had this fear most of her life, it was something she could overlook in the past because she encountered bridges uncommonly. When we moved to Jacksonville, Florida, however, it became something she had to confront daily. Because her work with new mothers requires her to drive all over the city to visit them in their homes, she had to push through that fear in order to do the job that she loves. At first, her heart would race, her fingers would grip the steering wheel, and she would instinctively slow her driving out of fear. With repeated exposure, though, her heart wouldn't speed up quite as much, her fingers would grip the wheel with a little less intensity, and she wouldn't reactively slow her driving. After repeated exposure, you would now never know that bridges were ever an issue for her. She drives at the same speed, with relaxed hands, and a calm heart when driving over bridges.

Despite her previous fear of driving over bridges, my wife does not have a fear of heights—that's my weakness. Although I only notice it while I'm on my own feet outside (not in a car or train or inside of a building, for instance), when I'm up high, my acrophobia kicks in and I feel weak-kneed and my stomach wants to do flip-flops. And guess what my wife loves most of all? A view. So, she loves to go outside on the top of the Empire State Building or climb bell towers on vacation to look at the city. I've overcome my fear enough to accompany her but lack the repeated exposure to facing this particular fear (I don't have to climb towers to do my job) means I still feel those butterflies in my stomach when I'm up high and looking down. But I'm there. I climb that tower and I share that view.

The same principle applies to our fear at work. We fear the uncertain future, impending irrelevance, the loss of our job, the disapproval of our superiors, and we may fear interacting with others outside of our sphere. While those fears lie unknown in your unconscious, you live a driftwood life. You must make your unconscious fears conscious to stop being adrift and be in control of your life and then take steps to overcome them. It won't happen all at once, just as my wife didn't overcome her fear of bridges overnight, and just as I still am overcoming my fear of heights, but each step we take is a step closer to getting in the boat.

Some organizations have cultures which are adversarial and create environments where people are looking out only for themselves despite others or even the business being hurt in the process. The interdepartmental rivalries in these organizations can be extreme and the technologist struggles to find firm ground. This is not only dangerous, but it is also complicated by our body producing a neurotransmitter called cortisol. Cortisol is responsible for the feelings of stress and anxiety and fear. It's the first stage of our fight or flight response. It increases our heart rate, makes us paranoid, and hyper-attunes our senses to look for danger. And it spreads to those nearby: If one person is stressed, soon others will be. The problem is that our jobs often inject a steady trickle of cortisol into our bloodstream. That's not how it's supposed to work: Cortisol should leave after danger, as you exhale deeply with relief. But the constant stresses of our jobs keep cortisol coming.

Cortisol counteracts the positive chemicals. It makes you less cooperative, altruistic, and generous, and more anxious, stressed-out, and fearful. And you impact everyone around you.

So, what should you do? Understand the unseen forces that are affecting your behavior and take steps to counteract them. Take steps to get more of those positive neurotransmitters by getting to know your co-workers, setting achievable goals, and praise yourself and others for a job well done. These all work against cortisol. Only when you take care of yourself will your neural transmitters work for you and not against you. Only then will you function well within the group.

Only then will functional leaders want you in the same boat.

TECHNICIANS

Chapter 18.

Three Steps to Elevate: How to Change Your Color

You have learned how to understand Green strategists, and also how to communicate as a Blue operator. But how do you move yourself, or someone else, from Red to Blue? Here's an example that walks through the process.

You're an IT manager in an aluminum manufacturing company. The company has been around for a long time, but recently landed a contract with a large automobile manufacturer who wants to use aluminum for its vehicles. We will say that the manufacturer is Audi in our story. As the IT manager, you want to have a Blue mindset. You aren't trying to be Green, because you're receiving and not giving direction. And you don't want to be viewed as Red, because there's no potential for advancement or job security as a tactician when operating in a Blue role.

Besides, you're a manager, so your role is clearly more than the tactical job of Red. Your frame of mind needs to be Blue.

So, you start thinking about the structure of your organization. You want to enable its goals, such as, "Fulfill our commitment to Audi." As you consider the last few years, you remember significant communications network failures at some of the 30 plants. You revisit those cases, study up on the problem and recommended solution, and go see the head of IT Infrastructure.

You sit in his large office and say, "Many of our plants have multiple single points of failure in their communication networks. We've been aware of this for a few years, but now that we have a new customer it's a greater challenge. We want to fulfill our commitment to Audi and avoid penalties. What kind of budget do we have to fix these single points of failure so we can deliver aluminum on time?" You hear the all-too-frequent answer, "The budget has no money set aside for that sort of project." Now what do you do?

You use my **three-step Elevate process** to help your boss think Blue instead of Red:

- The first step is **Turncoat**: Show your boss why he needs to switch sides. Share the Blue mindset of enablement and service, explaining that the IT team's goal is to enable the organization. You want your boss to become conscious to his fear so he can assess it as risk, the risk of misalignment with the strategists. Now, your boss may or may not be responsive to this approach. If not, you move on to Step 2.

- Step 2 is **Stump the Chump**: Am I recommending you call your boss a chump? No, that's just a memory aid, of course! You want to stump the chump by asking a pointed question (a type of pattern interrupt). For instance: "What happens when we are not shipping aluminum to Audi?" You hear back, "I'm not sure, but I know it's bad." That is a quintessential Red response. Any non-precise answer is Red and your boss is not behaving like a Blue operator who knows his actions enable or disable the organization. In that case, move on to step 3.

Step 3 Phone a Friend: You need to find a Blue person somewhere else in your organization. Look cross-functionally, maybe to the VP of Applications, Heather. You land a meeting with her and say, "I've been wondering. As you know, I run the communications network here, and I'm a little worried about my team. Are we doing our job in a way that enables our company? I have some concerns, so I need to ask you a question: What happens when we're not shipping aluminum to Audi?" Heather replies, "$10,000 a minute happens. Every minute we are not shipping to aluminum to Audi costs us $10,000." That is a Blue answer.

Now you have found a Blue person and gained an important piece of data. What other metrics do you need? Maybe you should ask, "How often have we had penalties this quarter?" She tells you, "Well, we're new to this automobile contract, and we've been able to negotiate less severe penalties since it's the beginning of the relationship, but this last quarter we had 48 hours of downtime. By the way, we'd love you to do a cause analysis, because we're pretty sure the downtime has to do with our communication network."

You say, "Wow, you're probably right. I've been looking at my own metrics and telemetry data and I saw those communication network outages in our plants. I didn't realize what impact that had on the applications it drove, on the processes required for you to both manufacture and ship aluminum to Audi. Now I'm starting to understand."

"Those communications network failures are really costly. Forty-eight hours of downtime, times sixty minutes an hour, times $10,000 a minute—that's $28.8 million in penalties this last quarter."

"Okay. Who else in this business would care? I think I know how to solve the problem, but I've been told there's no budget for this."

She says, "The Chief Risk Officer owns the relationship with Audi. Let's set up a lunch next week." You agree, set the date, and walk back to the VP of Infrastructure's office. You want to protect yourself and not let your boss think you're undermining him: "Hey, I just spoke with the VP of Apps, because I'm trying to figure out the risk associated with our communications network. Do you have any issues with that, or any questions you'd like me to ask your peer?" This should relieve your boss from worries that you'll throw him under the bus.

Next week you go to lunch with the CRO. You know his responsibility is clearly Green. You also know that he has people coming to him all day every day with alleged problems and proposed solutions, such that he's in a constant state of disbelief. His "reptilian" brain state is fully engaged, ready to disregard whatever you say (we will talk more on that, later). You will need to prompt him. I would recommend you say, "Thanks for meeting with me. I've been talking to our Red people and our Blue people." The CRO will respond, "What are you talking about? Do I need to call HR?" "No, no, no—let me tell you what that means."

PERFECT !

You just executed a successful pattern interrupt by surprising the CRO's expectations and disturbed him into asking a question. You continue, "Red people are internally, tactically focused. They provide the support to the Blue people in the organization. The Blue people are the enablers, the engine of growth, the ones who operate the business functions. Heather here, the VP of Apps, is Blue. Her job is to ensure that our applications have the logic required for you to be successful. As for you, you're Green. You provide the direction to our organization: vision, focus, culture."

GREEN
BLUE
RED

The CRO replies, "Wow, I love that. That's a great system to understand people."

Now you need to ask a validating question. You interrupted his pattern so he'd switch from reactive lower-order thinking to his frontal cortex—ask a question that requires higher processing. The VP of Apps gave you the validating information and you turn it into a question for the CRO. "I've heard from Heather, and want to validate, that every minute you're not shipping aluminum to Audi costs $10,000. Is that correct?" "Yes, that's correct."

"Okay, I have another question. Heather told me we've had 48 hours of outages in the last quarter. Is that correct?" "Correct." "I did some research after Heather told me that and discovered a group cause for most of those issues: our communications network. The current state of our network is that we have multiple single points of failure in the plant networks, which sometimes causes a stoppage of the applications required for us to run the processes required to ship aluminum. My team and I have identified the root causes of these outages. We are confident we can solve the issue and create a future state with a more reliable network, fewer outages, and greater confidence in meeting our commitment to Audi."

The CRO says, "That sounds great." You've brought him from disbelief, to interrupt, to engaged, to validating, to understanding, to current state, to future state. Now he asks the obvious question: "How much would solving the problem cost?" "Well, it's just slightly more than our penalty cost from last quarter: $30 million." "That's it?" "Yeah. Our problem is that we currently don't have that within our budget. We could try to budget that for next year or do something else." "We can't wait until next year. We need to move forward."

You ask the CRO to meet with your boss to get the go-ahead. Your boss may be surprised, perhaps even concerned, but if you have kept him in the loop he should recover quickly enough. Protect yourself from backlash by supporting your boss, trying to elevate him from Red to Blue.

In the end, the CRO finds the needed $30 million and you carry out the change. Network reliability increases, downtime decreases, and stoppages are a thing of the past. The CRO is happy because he's saving $28.8 million in penalties each quarter. The VP of Apps is happy because her applications are no longer crashing due to communications network issues. Your boss is happy because he gets credit for the change. And you're happy because you have enabled the business to meet its goals.

If you were Red before this, you are Red no longer. You've crossed the chasm to Blue. You played the "turncoat" card on yourself! Maybe you are still a mix of red and blue, like purple. That's okay! There is a continuum and you can have some leeway to practice. But you took an important first step and used your tactical skills to solve a problem and enable your organization.

You have become *relevant.*

Let's review the **three steps to Elevate** that we saw in the aluminum example. If you want to be Blue, you must elevate yourself using these three tools.

Turncoat > *RED MINDSET* > *BLUE*

Turncoat means you (and your team and your leadership) must ask, "How do we become enablers?" Your job is to handle the support function of the organization. How do you support the company's mission? That is turncoat; turning from red to blue, or perhaps purple as a midpoint.

Stump the chump

Second, you need to **stump the chump**. Start asking questions of people that you didn't ask before. Ask questions that are pertinent to the business and pertinent to you. Ask questions that connect the dots from tactics to operations to strategy. Remember value chaining? Coffee is not just about the bean. We need to connect it to what most people care about—the flavor and aroma and wake-up properties—and we do that through the process (say, a French Press). Tacticians care so much about the beans, but beans don't matter until you connect the dots. Ask connecting questions to stump chumps and get them to start thinking Blue.

Phone a friend

Phone a friend comes into play when you need help. In the Audi aluminum example, Heather the VP of Apps was the friend you needed. She connected you with the CRO (another friend), who provided the network upgrade funding. If you can't go straight up to your boss—because he's Red—you have to find a Blue person somewhere else in the company.

The cool thing about phoning a friend is that it reduces your risk. For a Red person, the primary risk is (1) being outsourced or (2) having your protector [i.e. boss] leave. By extending your network to a new friend, you reduce your risk—you have found another protector. That relationship also enables IT to ask better questions upward into the organization. Other times you can hire an outside consultant to credibly confirm your perspective, and that's phoning a friend too.

Those three steps are how you elevate.

Robert Schaffner's story:

> *I once held a one-day training seminar in Nuremberg for Bechtle, a large German B2B IT provider. The whole seminar went well, with the "Elevate" session being particularly well received. At the end of the seminar, I was felt happy because the attendees were pleased. Some people came up to me, thanked me for the presentation, and promised to implement what they had learned.*
>
> *Then I moved on to the next event in the next city. I forgot all about the Bechtle training until I returned to Bechtle a few months later to give a keynote address. (The address was titled "Learning from LEGO: Everything Is Awesome," which should make sense if you think back to the chapter on value chaining.)*
>
> *After the keynote, a person suddenly came up to me and said, "Hi Robert! Do you remember me?" I replied, "Yes, I remember you somehow—but from where?"*
>
> *He said, "My name is Eddy; I was at your Nuremberg training. You talked about the colors and said, 'You need to*

change your behavior.' And after your training I did change my behavior. The next day, I phoned a few customers and spoke in Blue language as much as I know how to do. And it really had an impact!

"Even more importantly, I started to communicate differently within my company. You won't believe it, but four weeks after your training, my management asked me, 'Eddy, you behave differently. What happened?' I told them your training gave me new ideas and a new way to communicate. Ultimately, they offered me a new job—instead of account manager, the sales lead for our region. Now I'm managing a whole sales team, and to be honest, it never would have happened had I not attended your training. Because I learned to speak Blue, I was successful with the customers, and now I have a more enjoyable and better-paid job. I'm pushing my people to adopt the ideas and practices from your training. So, thank you—what I learned had a huge impact on me."

You should be encouraged by this story. What you are learning *truly works*. Eddy implemented the "turncoat" Elevate strategy on himself. Before, he was thinking and acting like a typical Red person. After the training, he decided to start thinking and acting like a Blue person. That decision enhanced his professional well-being. Now, the effect in your life may not be quite so rapid or dramatic—but it will come.

3 Steps to Elevate
1. Turncoat (change perspective)
2. Stump the chump (value chain)
3. Phone a friend (get support)

Get in the Boat Whiteboard

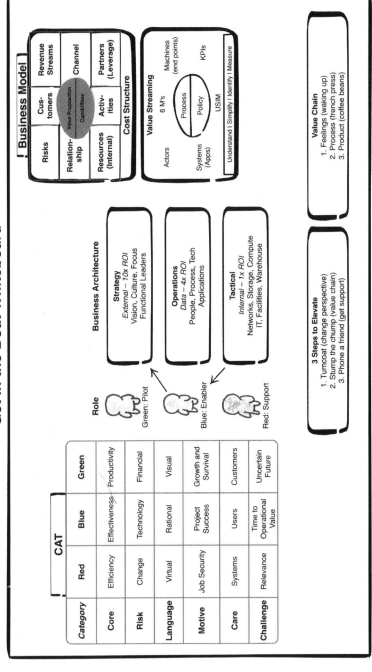

Business Model

Risks	Cus-tomers	Revenue Streams
Relation-ship	Value Proposition / Capabilities	Channel
Resources (Internal)	Activ-ities	Partners (Leverage)

Cost Structure

Value Streaming

Actors	6 M's	Machines (end points)
	Process	
Systems (Apps)	Policy	KPIs

USIM

Understand | Simplify | Identify | Measure

Business Architecture

Strategy
External – 10x ROI
Vision, Culture, Focus
Functional Leaders

Operations
Data – 4x ROI
People, Process, Tech
Applications

Tactical
Internal – 1x ROI
Networks, Storage, Compute
IT, Facilities, Warehouse

Role

Green: Pilot

Blue: Enabler

Red: Support

Value Chain
1. Feelings (waking up)
2. Process (french press)
3. Product (coffee beans)

3 Steps to Elevate
1. Turncoat (change perspective)
2. Stump the chump (value chain)
3. Phone a friend (get support)

CAT

Category	Red	Blue	Green
Core	Efficiency	Effectiveness	Productivity
Risk	Change	Technology	Financial
Language	Virtual	Rational	Visual
Motive	Job Security	Project Success	Growth and Survival
Care	Systems	Users	Customers
Challenge	Relevance	Time to Operational Value	Uncertain Future

Chapter 19.

Three Steps to Relevant Execution

Call your shot *— BE RELEVANT*
— BE CONFIDENT
— BE PERSISTENT

The first step to relevance is to be willing to **call your shot**. In 1932 at Wrigley Field in Chicago, a baseball player for the Yankees pointed his bat toward left field. The pitcher hurled the ball toward them, he swung his bat, and then he proceeded to hit the ball out of the park. That player was Babe Ruth. He called his shot and then he executed. Like the Babe, you must call your shot, because if you don't call your shot then when you hit your ball out of the park, *you're just lucky.*

Think about salespeople. They have a quota, and—if you haven't been in sales you might not know this—they themselves agree to their quota. That agreement between them and the business is a form of calling their shot.

We should do the same thing in technology. As leaders, we must predict our next action before we execute it, lest the strategists and operators think we got lucky. We don't want to be considered lucky! We want to be definite. To do that, we must call our shot.

You can do this in small ways, initially. Let's imagine that you're going to have a forklift migration, in which you completely replace an existing architecture with a new one. The first thing that you should do, is apply a change control update to whatever system your company uses and attend the meeting to discuss with confidence that your change will create a benefit and that your team has mitigated the associated risk. That is calling your shot and change control is built for it. (The other advantage of change control is that it allows you to make sure you are aligned with the rest of the organization before you act.) *You need to call your shot.*

Hit your mark

Calling your shot is not enough; you need to **hit your mark**. Let's say that you are an archer at a competition and have been assigned to Lane A. You stand in your lane, pull back your bow, release, and shoot your arrow straight into the bullseye—of the target in Lane B! What's your score? Zero. You executed, but not in the proper context.

We have that problem in technology. We often execute as if in a vacuum, and therefore we don't realize the context. Hitting any mark outside our lane is irrelevant. If you shoot a bullseye in the wrong target, you get zero—and that's exactly the value you get from the operators and strategists when you miss your mark, even though you think you hit it. You must operate within the framework of what your organization does. [NO MY ROLE]

Salespeople get paid by quota. They have various products and services to sell, with a quota for each, and on top of those quotas they might have *accelerators*. Accelerators are bonuses the company attaches to high sales for a certain product. Achieving the accelerator requires the salespeople to sell a lot of *one specific thing*. They could go beyond quota with every other product but still not get their accelerator. The strategists want the salespeople to be aligned with the organizational goals, so they give accelerators accordingly. As a salesperson, you must hit the mark to get your bonus. As a technologist, you must hit the mark to be trusted by the strategists.

Measure what matters

The last step to relevance is to **measure what matters**. During the first two steps, you have called your shot and executed flawlessly within the scope and context of your pledge. Now you must measure what matters—the key performance indicators (KPIs) that matter to your action. Our problem in technology is that we often measure arbitrary indicators that matter to us alone, like *how fast I can bring up a virtual machine*. But nobody else cares. You must measure something that matters *to the business*, to the mission, to whatever you're trying to accomplish. Establish a baseline prior when you call your shot, then measure what matters afterwards, and you will see the change. The delta (change) is your impact. Strategists like data and hard facts. When you call your shot, hit your mark, and measure what matters, they learn they can trust you to contribute to the organization's mission. That's the kind of person they want in the lead boat.

Now you know the three steps to relevant execution: ***call your shot, hit the mark, measure what matters.*** As you utilize these tools, you will find yourself moving towards a place of enablement. You are moving toward the lead boat, seeing the challenges ahead, understanding the strategists' concerns. And you are serving as the engine that enables the boat to follow the strategists' trajectory. The leaders say to "Go that direction!" and you enable the boat to obey.

We technologists are important, but our importance is not based solely on competency. Our importance is based on our ability to prioritize, execute within context, measure what matters, and enable the organization.

---

3 Steps to Relevance
1. Call your shot (no luck)
2. Hit your mark (prioritize)
3. Measure what matters (trust)

Get in the Boat Whiteboard

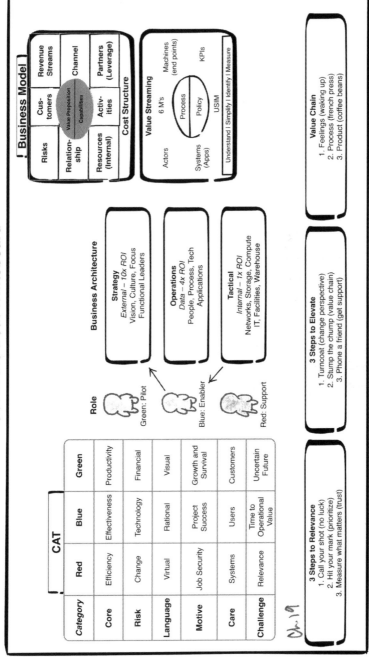

Business Model

Risks	Revenue Streams
	Cus-tomers
Relation-ship	Channel
Resources (Internal)	Activ-ities
	Partners (Leverage)

Value Proposition / Capabilities

Cost Structure

Value Streaming

Actors · 6 M's · Machines (end points)

Process

Systems (Apps) · Policy · KPIs

USIM

Understand I Simplify I Identify I Measure

Business Architecture

Strategy
External – 10x ROI
Vision, Culture, Focus
Functional Leaders

Operations
Data – 4x ROI
People, Process, Tech
Applications

Tactical
Internal – 1x ROI
Networks, Storage, Compute
IT, Facilities, Warehouse

Role

Green: Pilot

Blue: Enabler

Red: Support

CAT

Category	Red	Blue	Green
Core	Efficiency	Effectiveness	Productivity
Risk	Change	Technology	Financial
Language	Virtual	Rational	Visual
Motive	Job Security	Project Success	Growth and Survival
Care	Systems	Users	Customers
Challenge	Relevance	Time to Operational Value	Uncertain Future

Value Chain
1. Feelings (waking up)
2. Process (french press)
3. Product (coffee beans)

3 Steps to Elevate
1. Turncoat (change perspective)
2. Stump the chump (value chain)
3. Phone a friend (get support)

3 Steps to Relevance
1. Call your shot (no luck)
2. Hit your mark (prioritize)
3. Measure what matters (trust)

SECTION VI.

COMMUNICATE RELEVANTLY

Chapter 20.

Be Interested, Not Interesting

There has always been a focus on the art of speaking or communicating. Why is it an *art*? Webster defines art as, "The expression or application of human creative skill and imagination..." Have you ever been in a conversation and wondered if the person you were talking to was mentally checking out what was going on elsewhere in the crowd instead of focusing on your conversation? There is a reason. Have you ever given a public speech and wondered why people were looking at their smart phones instead of paying attention to your very important words? There is a reason.

First, there are at least two actors in every conversation; the speaker and the listener. The speaker tends to believe that everyone should have the same appreciation of the topic they are discussing as they do. That is the start of the disconnect in communication. This assumption can lead to misunderstanding and disinterest at best and total breakdown at worst. Isabel Briggs

Myers, the daughter of the famous mother-daughter team, Myers-Briggs, once stated, *"We cannot safely assume that other people's minds work on the same principles as our own. All too often, others with whom we come in contact do not reason as we reason, or do not value the things we value, or are not interested in what interests us."* Rarely will the technologist find other people outside of the IT field who are interested in what they have to say because they do not value the same things. Understanding this is the start to realizing why we aren't in the same boat and in making steps towards change.

Our next challenge is biological. The concept of the triune brain was developed by neuroscientist Paul MacLean in the 1960s and popularized Carl Sagan in the 1970s, who described the inner workings of the brain as being reptilian, roughly referring to the basal ganglia; paleo-mammalian, roughly referring to the limbic system; and neo-mammalian, roughly referring to the cortex. Although the triune brain was originally conceived to explain brain origins and is now outdated from an evolutionary perspective, it is still a very useful tool to illustrate communication methods.

The complex ideas that technologists have and which they desire to communicate are transmitted from the cortex. This is the part of the brain that controls important cognitive skills in humans, such as higher-level thinking and problem solving, emotional expression, memory, and the ability to delay reward and weigh consequences. It is the control system of our personality and our ability to communicate. This is part of the brain that is engaged when we deliver our presentation. Unfortunately, our listeners aren't always using the same brain functions to listen and there is often a disconnect due to this.

So much information is flowing these days that the brain just wants to discard everything. How many of your lectures from university can you remember? Probably not many. The ones that you do remember are because your professor used an interrupt to engage your brain. The brain gravitates toward the familiar while simultaneously ignoring it. If it is too familiar, we ignore it, if it is too unfamiliar, we discard it. In order to get someone's attention, we must appeal to the familiar while interrupting the pattern of inattention. Here are some examples of interrupts:

- In a movie trailer, the music and lack of action lull you into a sense of security before an abrupt action sequence.

- You're at a coffee shop when you hear breaking glass. You naturally stop your work or conversation and look toward the noise.

- The keynote speaker at a conference abruptly pauses for a full five seconds. You come back from whatever you were thinking about and focus on the speaker's next words.

- A comedian makes a pun by cleverly twisting words in a way you didn't expect. (Humor is one of the most common pattern interrupts.)

With the reptilian brain, it looks for both the familiar and the frightening so that it can either choose to ignore it as something safe, or pay attention to it as something unfamiliar, something which needs greater attention to discern whether or not it is threatening. A pattern interrupt is the ability to prompt the "reptilian brain" to send the information to the higher brain functions for review. The most effective tools in pattern interrupts are storytelling, humor, and sometimes even slight offense (a poke in the eye) as long as it is done with respect to the person, situation, and culture so that the receiver doesn't actually feel threatened.

As an example of mild offense, I'll share the story of a time when I was presenting to a team at a large New York financial around 10 years ago. One of the engineers told me before class that he expected me to be miming whatever the manufacturer had told me to say rather than giving accurate information and he felt like this was going to be a waste of his time. I promptly told him, "In the decade I have been representing this company, I have not lost my credibility and it's not going to happen today! You can sit down and listen or you can get up and leave." He loved my response, stayed, and was thoroughly engaged. This response worked with this particular gentleman in New York City. There are many other cultures and personalities that this would not be acceptable with, but it is our job as a communicator to be able to discern what is going to be culturally appropriate in each instance and gear our response toward that.

Obviously, these interrupts should be done with nuance and understanding of the local culture. What you can say as a pattern interrupt in London may not be acceptable to say in Jakarta.

Once I was communicating to a senior executive of a large manufacturer with whom we had done a lot of business. I came into the meeting with all of these great topics I wanted to discuss, as if I were the proverbial guy with the overcoat full of watches: "Here are many things I can sell you!" During the meeting, I told the executive all about the new projects we wanted to move forward with. Unbeknownst to me, her company had just experienced a security breach. She was hearing my ideas and thinking only about new security threats.

Now, I knew her business intimately. I thought I understood her needs. But I didn't really, all because I failed to sit and listen to her concerns before starting my spiel. After the security issue, she most wanted to learn more about the vulnerabilities in her organization. She wanted me to listen to her and offer solutions for that problem. To communicate more effectively, I should have focused on her concerns.

I learned from that conversation that it's not only important what you know—it's more important that you engage. When I was just 15 years old, I used to sell advertising door-to-door to small businesses. I would walk into these businesses, typically of 50 people or less, and talk to the owner. As a 15-year-old, I was not important and nothing I knew was important—the only important thing I had was *my interest in the owner.* You can call this principle *"Be interested, not interesting"* (BINI) and is a tidy way to think about active listening.

Active listening, where we are focused on being interested rather than interesting, removes the default filter we all use to filter others' words. We normally automatically assume that others use words as we would mean them or that they see the world as we do. That is often a false assumption. Listen and ask questions to probe and understand their perspective.

Every day we interact with people who do not reason as we reason, do not value the things we value, and are not interested in what interests us. In the world of IT, a tactician and a strategist communicate with distinct mannerisms, terminologies, and paradigms. Yes, even the words they say may have different meanings: "efficiency" to a tactician may not seem efficient to a strategist.

Specifically, for an example, if a tactician is going to talk to a strategist, then he or she needs to follow the BINI principle: **Be Interested, Not Interesting**. Why? Because there is really nothing about the nuts and bolts of the tactician's job that is interesting to a strategist. The tactician needs to be interested in them and their role, instead. The strategist's default mode is to *disbelieve and disregard* and your first countermeasure is to *be interested, not interesting*.

The second way you can help the strategist listen is to use a pattern interrupt. This could be a probing and insightful question, or a humorous one-liner. A person's manner of speaking or accent can be a beneficial pattern interrupt if it's understandable.

Chapter 21.

Value Mapping

Call me MR FAB

(handwritten annotation: — FEATURE — ADVANTAGE — BENEFIT)

How does one map their value, what they know, what they do, to their company's business needs? Robert Schaffner struggled with this for several years, mulling it over in his mind and collaborating with myself and others, before coming up with a solution that satisfied him, helped others, and had an impact. It's called "MR FAB".

Now, you may be thinking, "What on earth is that? Who is Fab and why are we calling him, 'Mr'?" Well, MR FAB is an acronym that Robert enhanced before teaching a session on business relevance in Paris. He was playing around with the letters "FAB," which is a common acronym standing for "Feature, Advantage,

Benefit". People have been using this acronym for years, saying, "Don't talk about features in your presentation; talk about benefits," because a feature is meaningless if it does not provide an advantage and the advantage is meaningless if it does not provide a benefit. Ultimately, we are seeking the benefit for our company, not a fancy widget.

→ FUNCTIONALITY

Feature: So, what exactly is a feature? A feature is a functionality in a product or a service. A feature of a large, front loading washing machine, for instance, might be a depth of 5.8 cubic feet. A feature of a printer might be a print resolution of 1200 x 1200 dpi.

→ VALUE IN THE DIFFERENTIATING ASPECT

Advantage: What is an advantage? Advantages are noted through comparison. The product or service may be compared to itself ("New and improved!") or compared to the way we use to do things in the past as opposed to the way we now do them today. We compare outwardly, looking at what our company's product does with what the competitor's product does. When we compare the difference, we should find some advantages over the other solution. So, the advantage to greater depth of 5.8 cubic feet over the average washing machine's depth of 3.3 cubic feet would be the ability to fit more laundry in the machine at a time. The advantage to a printer with higher resolution would be the greater clarity it provides.

Benefit: What is a benefit? A benefit is something that generates value for whomever is consuming the product or service. In our home example, the larger volume in depth, which leads to the capacity to fit in more laundry, produces the value of time savings—less time spent doing multiple loads of laundry. The benefit of higher resolution, leading to greater clarity, produces the value of visual appeal and the feeling of greater professionalism associated with that. The main consumer of technology solutions are the Blue and Green people, so you need to be asking yourself the question, "What intangible value are we providing them through our solution?" It is the *intangible value* that is the benefit!

That's FAB in a nutshell. Understanding FAB is a good starting point, but it is too generic. How so? Well, not everyone has the same values, as we discussed earlier with the different motivations of Red, Blue, and Green people, so not everyone will be incentivized by the same benefit. Robert realized, as he contemplated these things in his hotel room that night, that FAB was ready for a color extension! In doing so, he added "MR" to the front of FAB: Motivation and Risk.

Motivation: Each color, Red, Blue, Green, desires a different intangible benefit from your product. That means that we need to link motivation to FAB. What motivates them? What is their proverbial "carrot," what is their desire?

Risk: In most people's psyche, there is not only the carrot, but also the stick. Desire is the positive side of action and fear is the negative side. What risks are Red, Blue, and Green people are afraid of? What are their worries? You need to tailor your benefits to their negative emotions, as well as their positive.

The "MR" part of MR FAB varies depending on your function within the company. Different jobs are going to have different "gains," factors that drive motivation, and different "pains," factors that feed perceived risk. The pain and gain of a Red IT tactician is very different than the pain and gain of the Green CEO. Unless you put the correct motivation and risk together with the features, advantages, and benefits, you will not be able to have a meaningful conversation because you will be speaking a different language.

For example, we all have to give PowerPoint presentations from time to time. If you give similar presentations, you may not want to build a completely new PowerPoint for every session, so you might look at what you have and recycle some of your slides from a previous presentation, when applicable. Of course, the challenge is that each presentation should be built with a certain audience in mind—otherwise you might present Red slides to Green people.

Any time you build a presentation, you should run MR FAB through your mind: "Whom does this slide address? What motivation is it appealing to? What risk does it raise?" Create or adjust slides and edit text based on that analysis. It helps each presentation to be fresh and relevant to its intended audience. Value mapping is the ability to connect the dots between the Red, Blue, or Green person and what you provide them. You will find MR FAB is a great augmentation to traditional Value Mapping.

Value Map

How do you startle your hearers into focused attention so that you can have a rich, robust conversation? You do it with a pattern interrupt. Now, there are all kinds of ways to do pattern interrupts. Humor is one; mild offense is another; shock and awe (but not fear) is a third.

It is interesting what does not penetrate disbelief: information. Doling out information, with its facts, figures, statistics, and history does not penetrate disbelief. If it did, we would not see the same scenario played over and over on social media: Person 1 says, "I believe that xyz is great and I'm glad that it is happening!" Person 2 sees that and responds, typing back, "No! Xyz is terrible! Look at this website backing me up! Read the data! View the statistics!" Person 1 shoots back their own website data and no one changes their minds. Transmitting information, information, and more information does not convince people. Why? Because people already have too much information. They rarely want more content—especially content without context. That will fall on deaf ears every time.

Green strategists may be in a constant state of disbelief, but they desire to have *faith*. They want to believe. Annette Simmons, a keynote speaker and author, says that "People don't want more information. They are up to their eyeballs in information. They want *faith*—faith in you, your goals, your success, in the story you tell."[39]

The question is, how do you bring your hearers to the point of faith? How do you move them from not-believing to believing?

One method is *value mapping*. (We'll talk about another method later.)

Whenever you are going to communicate with somebody, you must use a pattern interrupt to get past the part of their brain that wants to discard what it doesn't find important and worthy of attention. Value mapping is a systematic way of doing that.

Let's make sure we keep things straight:

- **Value chaining** is connecting the dots from Red to Blue to Green. In the coffee example, it is connecting dots from the bean to the French press to the aroma.

[39] Annette Simmons, *The Story Factor: Inspiration, Influence, and Persuasion through the Art of Storytelling* (Cambridge, MA: Perseus Publishing, 2002), 3.

- **Value streaming** is diving into a process to understand it, improve it, and impact the operations of the whole organization. This is where the precision of the organization exists.

- **Value mapping** is working to understand someone's *job, gain, and pain* before you try to get them to buy into a solution.

A value map has two components: the *customer profile* and the *solution map*. Together, those make a value map.

Customer profile

Why is a customer profile important to communication? It is important because if you do not understand someone's job, what they count as a gain, and what pain they want to avoid, you will not speak to them in a relevant way.

Let's say you want to get buy-in from the head of sales on a project. Talk about programming, routers, and digitalization and you'll be ignored very quickly. The head of sales is not concerned about those things because that's not their job.

Additionally, knowing their gain and pain is important. The easiest way to determine gain is to ask one question: "What does a good day look like?" Meaning, "What things must happen for this to be a good day at work for you?" You will hear various answers. Maybe, "Higher-ups think that my work matters." Or, "I receive a promotion for excellent performance." People define gains differently.

Also ask, "What does a bad day look like?" Most employees can answer this question easily. Their workload is overwhelming, clients are upset, partners aren't cooperating, and their attempted solutions keep failing.

In Chapter 1 of this book, we discussed a booked called *"The Phoenix Project"*. There are a few characters in the book that align very well to the concepts of *"Get in the Boat"*. As discussed in chapter 1, Brent Geller was an incredibly talented tactician, but struggled with priority and relevance. He was also unhappy and struggled with his place in the organization. He was the Red person. The most important character of "The Phoenix Project" was the protagonist Bill Palmer. Bill had been working in mid-range systems which had become the back waters of IT. These systems were no longer the star of the IT show, but they were always operational and Parts Unlimited needed stability. At the request of potential new board member, Erik Reid, they promoted Bill to VP of IT Operations. Eric is Bill's mentor and forces Bill to face the challenges of managing an IT organization head on. Bill is Blue and through his struggles he confronts many IT failures, dysfunctional behaviors from the C-Suite, and through it all successfully navigates the IT organization to relevance and ultimately saves the company.

The other important character in the book is Steve Masters. Steve had been an operator most of his career and for the past few years had been the CEO of Parts Unlimited. He was unsuccessful in this role, partly due to sea-changes in his industry, but also his inability to move from Blue to Green. If you needed to navigate this organization and to provide solutions that would resonate, how would you do it?

The first step is understanding the people and what makes them tick. We use customer profiles to do this.

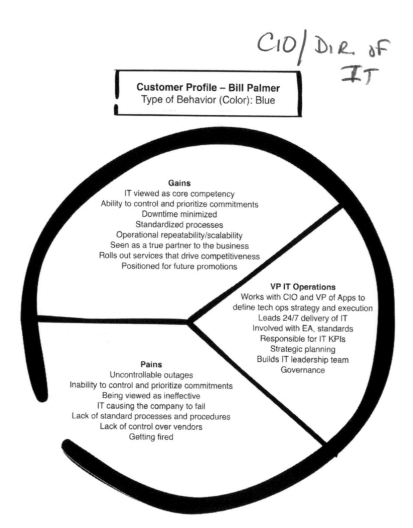

CIO / DIR. oF IT

Customer Profile – Bill Palmer
Type of Behavior (Color): Blue

Gains
IT viewed as core competency
Ability to control and prioritize commitments
Downtime minimized
Standardized processes
Operational repeatability/scalability
Seen as a true partner to the business
Rolls out services that drive competitiveness
Positioned for future promotions

VP IT Operations
Works with CIO and VP of Apps to
define tech ops strategy and execution
Leads 24/7 delivery of IT
Involved with EA, standards
Responsible for IT KPIs
Strategic planning
Builds IT leadership team
Governance

Pains
Uncontrollable outages
Inability to control and prioritize commitments
Being viewed as ineffective
IT causing the company to fail
Lack of standard processes and procedures
Lack of control over vendors
Getting fired

This first profile is for Bill Palmer, the head of IT for Parts Un-limited. The right segment of the profile contains his job description, while the segments on the left hold gains and pains. Read through Bill's profile to get an idea of what he wants to achieve.

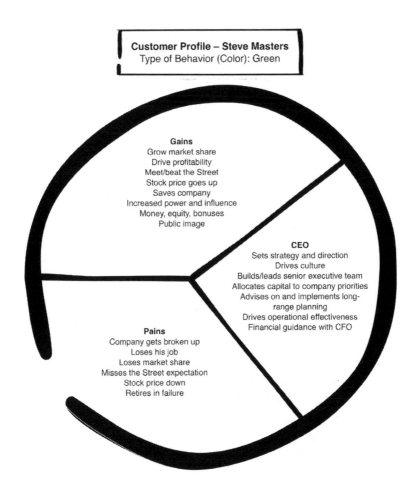

Customer Profile – Steve Masters
Type of Behavior (Color): Green

Gains
Grow market share
Drive profitability
Meet/beat the Street
Stock price goes up
Saves company
Increased power and influence
Money, equity, bonuses
Public image

CEO
Sets strategy and direction
Drives culture
Builds/leads senior executive team
Allocates capital to company priorities
Advises on and implements long-range planning
Drives operational effectiveness
Financial guidance with CFO

Pains
Company gets broken up
Loses his job
Loses market share
Misses the Street expectation
Stock price down
Retires in failure

The second profile is for Steve Masters, the CEO of Parts Unlimited. You'll notice that his gains and pains are at a different level than Bill's. Why? Because Steve is Green while Bill is Blue. Steve is a strategist who is constantly thinking about the company as a whole. Bill is charged with executing IT projects.

You want to communicate well with others in your organization. You want to know how to influence them. To do that, you must figure out their job, their gains, and their pains.

Solution map

You need someone to buy into your proposal. Since you have taken the time to identify their job and gains and pains, your next step is to develop a solution map.

The last chapter of "*The Phoenix Project*" narrates an IT initiative called "Project Narwhal," which was an upgrade to their Material Requirements Planning (MRP) solution. Parts Unlimited had outsourced their MRP solution, but now they needed to perform substantial upgrades. Bill Palmer (the head of IT) and Steve Masters (the CEO) decided with their teams that the best solution was to break the contract early and insource MRP. Then they could upgrade the data center and integrate the MRP with the order system.

Here's the solution map for Project Narwhal.

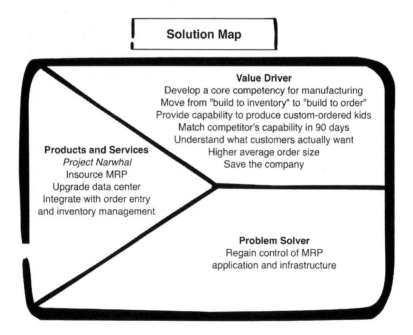

Solution Map

Value Driver
Develop a core competency for manufacturing
Move from "build to inventory" to "build to order"
Provide capability to produce custom-ordered kids
Match competitor's capability in 90 days
Understand what customers actually want
Higher average order size
Save the company

Products and Services
Project Narwhal
Insource MRP
Upgrade data center
Integrate with order entry
and inventory management

Problem Solver
Regain control of MRP
application and infrastructure

The solution map answers the question, "How will this solution provide value and fix our problem?" For Bill Palmer, Project Narwhal helped him regain control over a crucial asset. That problem *solver* relieved his *pain* of not having control over outside vendors. Project Narwhal also caused other leaders in the business to esteem IT more highly. That *value driver* links to Bill's *gain* of having IT perceived as a core competency.

For Steve Masters, Project Narwhal drove profitability (a *gain*) by matching competitor capabilities and offering the customization features customers desired (*value drivers*). Regaining control of the MRP application and infrastructure (*problem solver*) averted the risk of the company being broken up—and of him losing his job (*pains*).

The value drivers of the solution link with the gains of the people involved, and the problem solver alleviates their pain. That is exactly how a value map is supposed to work.

To sum up, a value map has two components: a customer profile and a solution map. One is a profile of the person you are trying to work with to understand their need, and the other is the solution you propose. You "map" the value driver to the person's gain, and you map the problem solver to their pain. That's value mapping.

The value map provides the content and context for a meaningful conversation or, in order words, a great message or story. A good message or story is one of the best pattern interrupts and is one of the best ways to positively influence your business leaders.

Messaging

Good communication and messaging can make sense of chaos. Have you experienced any chaos recently? IT personnel are best friends with chaos; functional leaders are, too. Good communication makes sense of chaos by establishing structure to our messaging. Inside messages, people have a role and a purpose. Good communication can bring down barriers and everyone loves a good message.

Once you have the proper perspective, understanding that you are not a lone wolf but a team player, you will want to seize opportunities to communicate with Green and Blue people. The form of communication that will be most beneficial to you is telling good stories. As a wise person once said, "In a complicated world, whoever tells the best stories wins."[40]

What do I mean by "telling good stories"? I don't mean creating works of fiction but conversing with your colleagues through humor and compelling antidotes that will bring them to a full state of engagement. They will no longer be bored by our tech speak, but fully involved in our meaningful conversation.

It would be nice if we all had a natural knack at delivering messages that resonated. Sadly, though some of us are naturally excellent storytellers, most of us are not. I'm decent, but I'm certainly not as skilled as many others. For "the rest of us," how do we effectively communicate in a way that helps us persuade others?

---

[40] I have been unable to find who first said this, though it has been attributed to film director James Cameron.

English has never been my strongest subject. Although I never enjoyed writing essays, the "three-point essay" format got me through the school requirements, following a specific method to get my message across until it became more natural. Messaging is similar in that we non-experts need a simple methodology to get started. Then, with additional practice, we will gradually improve the more we do it.

As you think about preparing your own messages, here are a few questions that will provide you structure to communicate in an interesting way.

Who is your audience?

Every message has an audience. Earlier in this book, we used the CAT tool to evaluate what people of each Color care about; you can fill in your audience's profile with those results. The details you choose to include for an audience of Red tacticians are necessarily different from those you include for Green strategists or for Blue operators.

Why are you communicating?

We have many potential motivations. Are you trying to influence your audience toward a course of action? Are you endeavoring to build team camaraderie? What are you trying to do?

What is the risk?

Most people react to risk. Do we know our audience's risk? That is where the CAT tool is very useful. If you are communicating to one of your senior leaders, their risk will be financial or compliance based. When messaging, confront the risk of the audience head on. Mitigate that risk, so they not only know you have a workable solution, but that you care about what concerns them.

What is your role?

What is your role in the conversation? As we discussed earlier, it is critically important to be interested, not interesting. Be an active listener. Decide if your role is to motivate, negotiate, or convince your audience. Our role should direct the type of questions and arguments that we will make.

Where is the conflict?

Most people believe that conflict and tension are bad things, but the reality is that conflict is an incredibly useful and needed tool as a catalyst for change. While avoiding interpersonal conflict, we must demonstrate the tension in our message, which is really just an illumination of what is going on under the surface. This allows us to motivate or convince our audience to work with us on a solution to the problem. Without the tension, the audience may not be as engaged as you need them to be.

What is your big idea?

When you are delivering a message, it needs to contain a central thought that matters to your audience. This is the theme of the conversation. Are you trying to help a Green person grow their business? Then that is your big idea! Are you trying to help a Blue person improve a process? Then that is your big idea! Your big idea must be clear and it must matter to your audience.

What is the emotion?

Messages that appeal to our emotions will resonate and be remembered. Emotional messages are meaningful.

Conversation Example

Here is an example of a conversation you might have, with notations illustrating the tools we have been discussing. In our example, George is the managing director and John is the head of technology:

John: "Hey George, thank you for your time today. A couple of weeks back I asked you, "What does a good day look like?" **[know your audience]** *You told me, "A good day for me is when our company flawlessly executes the integration of our acquisitions and streamlines our processes and cost and we are able to report top line earning growth and higher than expected profitability on our company's analyst call at the end of the quarter."* **[what is the risk]** *You then let me know that this hasn't happened in over four years. Our entire IT leadership took this to heart. If we continue to be out of step with you and your business leaders, this poor performance will not only continue but worsen.* **[what role, why are we communicating]**

"We've determined that acquisitions change our company's business model and that given the volume of acquisitions, we

need to radically improve the on-boarding of these new company resources and capabilities. We believe IT can IMPACT the goal of rapidly on-boarding these new acquisitions through two new initiatives: end-user computing and data center consolidation. **[big idea]** *Our end user computer initiative would make sure that these newly acquired employees have all of the tools they require when they need them. We would reduce the current time to provision workspace environments from two weeks to four hours. Data center consolidation would provide integration of all of these data center assets 10 times faster than we have historically delivered.*

"George, so far, are we on the right track? I just want to make sure to validate our assumptions that we made through examining our business model and business processes." **[emotion]**

George: "Absolutely! This is definitely top of mind for me! Continue."

John: "We have two new projects that underpin these initiatives. The first project is Virtual Desktop that provides instant access based on user credentials to all authorized applications wherever our newly acquired employees reside. This project allows the end user to be in any part of the world, which is something we feel is important, given our global growth. Also, they will be able to use any device to securely connect to our environment. If we acquire a company in Saudi Arabia tomorrow, our new employees will be operational as soon as the deal closes.

"The second project is a data center cloud project that consolidates all of our data and application resources into one, virtual facility. This will allow our newly acquired application resources to be integrated into our existing environment within days – not months. George, I'm sure you remember how long it

took us to integrate with the new Japanese acquisition – forever. [**conflict**] *With our new system, we would have improved the on-boarding of that new company by six months, which is 10x faster. George, the good news is that these changes will be done with the same budget that has already been allocated for this year! I know you and our CFO had planned to reduce our overall budget, but we think that these changes merit keeping the funds where they are. What do you think?"*

George: "Outstanding! What I love is that you directly connected the dots from the risks of our business to the technology projects that we need to mitigate those risks! I also love the fact that you are not hoping for these results but declaring them ahead of time – that's what we need from you! How did you change?" [**emotion**]

John: "George, I'm not sure how much longer we could have gone without change, but we read a few of the right books, started to research our business and others in our industry, and worked closely as a team to align our efforts with the functional leaders of our business. It wasn't one of us – it was all of us."

George: "Are you and some of your valuable team members available to go to an offsite executive council meeting next week? We are making some business decisions that are too critical to make without your team's insight." [**In the Boat**]

Meaningful Communication

If you consistently understand your audience, their gains, pains and job roles, and target your words to them in a way that they understand, you will reduce friction. If you can target your solution to your audience's specific needs and message that solution to them in a way that is easily digestible, you will reduce friction and they will appreciate you. If your story is full of context, humor, tension and emotion, it will not only provide you with an extremely useful pattern interrupt, but also dramatically reduce the friction in your organization. In fact, an incredibly talented tactician that can connect the dots between the business need and the technology requirement in a way that is interesting and compelling will always be invited to be in the boat.

Chapter 22.

Conclusion

I first started this journey because during the course of my interactions with businesses and business leaders, I couldn't help from noticing a disturbing paradox: Technology is more important than it has ever been, yet technologists are still divorced from the business. The solution? Technologists need to get in the boat!

Throughout this book, we've used a narrow lens to look at these disconnects. Some of them have taken years to form and others are structural, some are psychological and sociological, some of these are due to our training and our job roles. While all of these reasons must be understood, they should not prevent us from success. What's made us successful in the past is not guaranteed to even sustain us in the future. The rate of change has accelerated to an extreme pace and there is no end in sight. We now need everyone to see the challenges and risks simultaneously. The business cannot afford disconnects any longer. Our IMPACT framework is designed to address this head-on.

When you are looking to change, I have found it best to think of the Pareto Rule, more commonly known as the 80/20 rule. The daily activities that you must do, the tactical work that consumes most of your time, should still represent at least 80% of your time. Those are the table stakes required for you to not only keep your job but keep the lights on. Even though this 80% is required, it will generate you the least amount of return; people assume that your tactical work will be done and there are no congratulations for what is expected. That said, the other 20% or less of your time will be the time spent on being strategic and challenging yourself and your organization to have material IMPACT. In fact, that strategic 20% will generate over 80% of your success, rewards, and return.

This strategic component is what we've been talking about for this entire book:

How do you connect more effectively with business leaders that often perceive the world differently than you?

How do we ask questions that can really go deep, probing the actual problem to determine root cause?

Where do our business goals and initiatives come from?

How do we connect the dots from what we do to what the business actually needs?

That is what we have learned and much more throughout this book.

The IMPACT framework is straightforward; however, it still may not be clear where to start. There is a reason for this! We intentionally designed our framework to be useful to a wide spectrum of people. Some have been at this for a very long time and others not so long, some have been working for incredibly large organizations that may have major silos and others may be employed at smaller organizations that often work in the same room with others in their business. We are not in the same place. There are over 20 tools that are presented in this book, but where should you start? Here is the secret: you are already great at what you do! Our goal is to improve your communications, improve your business acumen, and ultimately earn you the right to be in the boat.

One of the common mistakes that is often made is trying to apply all the new tools into our work life simultaneously. That is difficult and quite frankly impossible for most of us to achieve. Most critically, however, we won't have any insight into the IMPACT of each of the individual changes. It is best to baseline our current situation through metrics; how many "kudos" do we get from the business today, or conversely, how often are we or our organization complained about, etc. Decide what you are going to change – call your shot! Then we can apply a single change, such as implementing value chaining in our workflow. We realize that the tangible things we do have little importance in themselves and we must connect the dots to what our business leaders are trying to achieve, such as customer happiness. We realize that we can use technology through the process, like the customer service process, to directly impact a key indicator, such as customer satisfaction. Customer satisfaction directly relates to our customer's happiness with our product or service. Our flawless execution in using technology to IMPACT this process, hitting the mark, is required for the business to trust us. After successful implementation, you measure what matters and compare that to the original baseline, asking yourself, "Did we move the needle?" Once it is clear that you had IMPACT, do it again with even more clarity. Once you have gained proficiency at value chaining, p.49 you can move on the next area of interest, such as color coding your colleagues so that you know where their interests lie. Rinse and repeat.

Once, Robert presented concepts from this book to a group of system integrators in Indonesia. The group consisted of about half salespeople and half solution engineers. Interestingly, in countries like Indonesia, salespeople see themselves as relationship owners—they are primarily focused on the relationship with the customer and not the solutions that they sell. They often think that this relationship is enough, that knowing more about their customer's business or their own solutions is for others to worry about. Their idea of selling is, "I know someone and that's why I am important." The solution engineers, who are much more technically minded, do the heavy lifting.

A few hours into the seminar, we began working on business models from the top down. We asked, "What do these specific customers care about?" The audience became very engaged.

In Indonesia, people usually arrive late because of traffic and want to leave early because of traffic. These people arrived late, but once they began working on their customers' business models, they didn't want to leave. At 8:00 p.m. they were still discussing their customers with Robert and his team, drilling down into use cases and processes.

They felt like Robert had given them a crystal ball! Finally, they understood what their customers actually cared about. They had conversation points for their next meeting. Better yet, the salespeople and solution engineers were working together to understand their customers – they were in the same boat. Both halves of the audience understood that they needed each other to capitalize on this tremendous opportunity they had never discovered before!

That's a small example with a big point: The concepts in this book work anywhere in the world. Sure, you can adjust details because of culture and language. But apply the main concepts around the globe and you will succeed.

My goal in this book has been to show IT tacticians a way to become relevant, impactful enablers. I want IT tacticians across the world to partner with Green strategists and fellow Blue enablers from other departments. I want technologists to tremendously impact the results of their organization.

I want you to speak Blue.

I want you to be interested, not interesting.

I want you to get in the boat. We need you there.

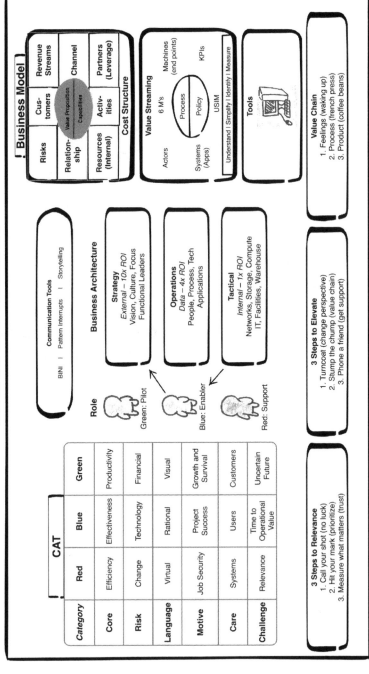

Reference

Remember

Here's a visual summary of this entire book. Refer to it for a quick reminder of what you've learned.

Read

Time to pick up some reading! Here are the most significant books that have influenced how I think about getting in the boat.

- ✓ *The Phoenix Project* by Gene Kim, Kevin Behr, and George Spafford
- *Start with Why* by Simon Sinek

- *The Three Signs of a Miserable Job* by Patrick Lencioni (recently reprinted under the title *The Truth About Employee Engagement*)
- *The Five Dysfunctions of a Team* by Patrick Lencioni
- *The 7 Habits of Highly Effective People* by Stephen Covey
- *Competitive Advantage* by Michael Porter
- *Business Model Generation* by Alexander Osterwalder
- *Blue Ocean Strategy: How to Create Uncontested Market Space and Make the Competition Irrelevant* by W. Chan Kim and Renée Mauborgne
- *The Power of Habit* by Charles Duhigg
- *The Story Factor* by Annette Simmons
- *The Hero with a Thousand Faces* by Joseph Campbell

Reach Out

If you want to go deeper with us, we have a number of ways to do that globally in a number of languages. The key to finding us is our website: www.intheboat.com. Here are our offerings:

- **KEYNOTE:** compelling stories and anecdotes that excite and motive your organization to change. We can conduct these sessions in large conventions or more intimate gatherings. The focus is always giving your team food for thought.

- **IMPACT:** collaborative workshop focused on the IMPACT framework to give your team a common language to systematically IMPACT your organization and to be relevant with your business leaders.

- **INTUITION:** coaching workshop using Six Sigma and Lean methods to align your projects to your customer's or your own business goals and initiatives. This workshop is project-focused using value chaining as a key tool for alignment.

- **RETOOL:** coaching workshop using Lean methods to understand your processes in a way that will allow your technology projects to have material IMPACT. This workshop is process-focused using value streaming as a key tool for digital transformation.

Acknowledgments

This book has been a journey, a labor. Many people along the way have helped us gain new insight and perspective that has made this book possible.

In order to get these concepts on paper, Robert and I enlisted the support of some extremely talented editors and writers to allow our concepts to be clear and digestible. Chrissy Bodin, Jae Harrison, and Caleb DeLon all did a fantastic job. I am deeply appreciative and especially thankful for Chrissy, whose many hours of patience, editing, re-reading, pushing me to clarify my thoughts, and refining my words, made this book possible. Dave Yeary, Justin Brady, and Alexander Bauman, thank you for sharing your stories and allowing our book to ring true.

I'm grateful for my colleagues Robert Schaffner and Michael Pohl who have been on this journey with me the past five years. We created the IMPACT framework together.

Many thanks go out to the individuals who added important elements and influenced our understanding: Paul Teel, Dave Liebman, Chris Neill, Kraig Schripsema, Terry Jenkins, JB Feeney, Bentley Curran, Jeff Klaubert, and Alexander Bauman.

We are very grateful to NetApp who provided the initial platform to discuss our program, Elevate. I would like to specifically thank the individuals who have helped us directly: Peter Howard, Dave Yeary, Deb Sperling, and Pete Friedman.

Thank you to Cisco's Channel organization and their leader for the Americas, Rick Snyder, who provided a wonderful conduit to grow these concepts through our IMPACT program. We appreciate all of the great Cisco partner resellers, partner account managers, and channel engineers who have been a part of the IMPACT success.

Cisco's technology (IT) organization and one of their leaders, Lance Perry, have given us good outlook into how our methodology impacts end user organizations. Special thanks to Lance, Mandy Knotts, Katty Coulson, Colin Seward, and Bram Van Spaendonk. It's been a pleasure to work with such a talented team who are so closely aligned with their business leaders.

We had some incredibly dedicated reviewers who provided much-needed perspective and great insight. Their feedback was invaluable and the changes we made based off of their suggestions have improved this work. Thank you to Dave Yeary for your encouragement and your detailed edits – it really helped that your mother was an English teacher! Thank you George Curtis, Justin Brady, and Paul Flig for being part of my Olympians program and for your thoughts and suggestions. Adam Braunstein and Cal Braunstein, I really appreciate your approach to putting business into technology. Jim French and Frank D'Agostino, we've been on similar journeys for many years – thank you for your encouragement and support throughout this project. Katty Coulson, your perceptive understanding of the many different types of people in IT has really added great value. Bill Bell, I am grateful for your multiple reviews of this book throughout its creation. Your programming background provided a much-needed lens to our work. Thank you to Louis Bodin for your careful review and edits. Finally, I want to express my gratitude to Lance Perry. Lance not only reviewed the book, but provided the forward. Thank you, Lance.

REVIEW WHITEBOARDS

About Pat and Robert

Pat Bodin started his career over 30 years ago as a Certified Public Accountant. After a few years as a CPA, he moved into the growing area of open computing. His technology career had him working with Lockheed Martin, Turner Broadcasting, and Cisco Systems. In 2003, Pat saw an opening in the education market to create an organization that demonstrated competency, experience, and know-how. Firefly became wildly successful and Pat sold it in 2012. Since then, Pat's interest has been in business relevance and continuous improvement. Pat lives with his family in Florida.

Robert Schaffner is a native Austrian and has lived and worked in Austria, Germany, Australia, and currently makes his home in Singapore. He started his career as a technologist 25 years ago at Siemens. In 2006, he co-founded Avodaq, a German IT system integrator. He co-founded the collaboration software company, Andtek, in 2011, which he later sold. Robert's passion is teaching leaders, sales teams, and organizations how to have impact on individuals, organizations, and society.

Bibliography

"How Packaging Gives Apple's Buyers a Sensory Experience that Reinforces Brand." Personalics. Last modified 2016. Accessed November 13, 2017. https://www.personalics.com/2016/02/03/sensory-design-packaging/.

"Retail Price of Milk (Fresh, Whole, Fortified) in the United States from 1995 to 2016 (in U.S. Dollars per Gallon)." Statista Inc. Last modified 2016. Accessed November 13, 2017. https://www.statista.com/statistics/236854/retail-price-of-milk-in-the-united-states/.

"What Are the Driving Forces of PESTLE Analysis?" ToughNickel. Last modified 2016. Accessed November 13, 2017. https://toughnickel.com/business/What-is-PESTLE-analysis.

Al Azhari, Muhamad. "Ride Sharing Apps Change the Face of Jakarta's Busy Streets." PT Jakarta Globe Media. Last modified 2016. Accessed November 13, 2017. http://jakartaglobe.id/news/ride-sharing-apps-change-face-jakartas-busy-streets/.

BusinessDictionary.com. "Channel." WebFinance, Inc. Last modified Accessed November 13, 2017. http://www.businessdictionary.com/definition/channel.html.

Company, The Coca-Cola. "2016 Annual Report on Form 10-K." The Coca-Cola Company. Last modified 2016. Accessed November 13, 2017. http://www.coca-colacompany.com/content/dam/journey/us/en/private/fileassets/pdf/investors/2016-AR-10-K.pdf.

Covey, Stephen R. *The Seven Habits of Highly Effective People.* 25th Anniversary ed. New York: Simon & Schuster, 2013.

Gillis, Tom. "Competing With Incumbents: Finding Your 10x." Forbes Media LLC. Last modified 2011. Accessed January 7, 2018. https://www.forbes.com/sites/tomgillis/2011/12/27/competing-with-incumbents-finding-your-10x/--17ac6b9d4940.

Govindarajan, Vijay and Hylke Faber. "How Companies Escape the Traps of the Past." Harvard Business Publishing. Last modified 2016. Accessed November 13, 2017. https://hbr.org/2016/04/how-companies-escape-the-traps-of-the-past.

Green, Dennis. "It's War: Walmart Is Telling Vendors to Stop Using Amazon's Cloud." Business Insider. Last modified 2017. Accessed November 13, 2017.

http://www.businessinsider.com/walmart-tells-its-tech-providers-to-stop-using-amazon-services-2017-6.

Jung, C.G. "Quotes." Goodreads Inc. Last modified Accessed November 13, 2017. https://www.goodreads.com/author/quotes/38285.C_G_Jung.

Langner, Christopher. "Uber, Disrupted." Bloomberg L.P. Last modified 2016. Accessed November 13, 2017. https://www.bloomberg.com/gadfly/articles/2016-04-15/uber-disrupted.

Lencioni, Patrick. *The Five Dysfunctions of a Team: A Leadership Fable.* San Francisco: Jossey-Bass, 2002.

Marder, Diana. "Flash: The True Story Of Lightning Bugs." Chicago Tribune. Last modified 1985. Accessed November 13, 2017. http://articles.chicagotribune.com/1985-08-18/news/8502230870_1_lightning-bugs-flash-abdomen.

Mehta, Sandeep. "Nokia R&D Spending – A Lesson in Portfolio Balancing." InspiRD. Last modified 2011. Accessed November 13, 2017. http://inspird.com/2011/02/15/nokia-r-spending-lesson-in-portfolio/.

O'Brien, Kevin J. "Nokia's New Chief Faces Culture of Complacency." The New York Times Company. Last modified 2010. Accessed November 13, 2017. http://www.nytimes.com/2010/09/27/technology/27nokia.html?_r=1&hp.

Porter, Michael E. "How Competitive Forces Shape Strategy." *Harvard Business Review* 59, no. 2 (1979): 137–45. Accessed November 13, 2017. https://hbr.org/1979/03/how-competitive-forces-shape-strategy.

Reuters. "Computer Beats Chinese Master in Ancient Board Game of Go." Telegraph Media Group Limited. Last modified 2017. Accessed November 13, 2017. http://www.telegraph.co.uk/news/2017/05/24/computer-beats-chinese-master-ancient-board-game-go/.

Sheely, Eugene. "The Winner Effect: How Success Affects Brain Chemistry." Gamification Co. Last modified 2014. Accessed November 13, 2017. http://www.gamification.co/2014/02/21/the-winner-effect/.

Simmons, Annette. *The Story Factor: Inspiration, Influence, and Persuasion through the Art of Storytelling.* Cambridge, MA: Perseus Publishing, 2002.

Slater-Thompson, Nancy and Slade Johnson. "The World's Nine Largest Operating Power Plants Are Hydroelectric Facilities." U.S. Department of Energy. Last modified 2016. Accessed November 13, 2017. https://www.eia.gov/todayinenergy/detail.php?id=28392.

Team, Mind Tools Content. "Porter's Value Chain." MindTools. Last modified Accessed November 13, 2017. https://www.mindtools.com/pages/article/newSTR_66.htm.

81195916R00141

Made in the USA
Lexington, KY
12 February 2018